TORAH TOC

THE BOOK

CREATED BY JOEL LURIE GRISHAVER

TORAH AURA PRODUCTIONS

First Edition

STUDENT INTRODUCTION

When I was a kid, I spent a lot of time doodling on the back of dittoed handouts they always want you to take home from school, and the margins of old homework assignments. I did it often, because I just wanted to figure out how something might look, or because I wanted to create my version of something I read. Since then, I've done a reasonable job of growing up and the doodling has turned into a way of earning a living - drawing cartoons to go with the curriculum materials I write. A few years ago, I was working for the Los Angeles Hebrew High School, and I began doing a thing called TORAH-TOONS. I'd draw these huge poster sized drawings of the weekly TORAH PORTION, and hang them on clothes-lines during the service. When we started TORAH AURA PRODUCTIONS, TORAH TOONS became a media series. Now, TORAH-TOONS is a book. Just like the first doodles I used to do in class, TORAH-TOONS is my way of figuring out how things in the TORAH might look, and a way of working out my own version of what the portions mean. Have the same fun with it - we did in producing it, draw your own doodles and figure out your own versions.

CHAZAK, CHAZAK V'NIT-CHAZEIK: The Gris.

TEACHER'S INTRODUCTION

Parshat Ha Shavua (studying the weekly Torah Portion) is an important Jewish process. It does many things. It takes the Jew on a annual journey through the entire Torah. It creates a background through which all kinds of major Jewish issues, themes and ideas are considered and reconsidered. And, perhaps most importantly, weekly study of the parsha creates a special sense of community - allowing participants to share their own insights and reactions. TORAH-TOONS is a curriculum package which tries to create the process of parshat ha-shavua for students who don't live in the mileau of the TORAH.

TORAH-TOONS II is a set of 36 slide-tape segments designed to provide a single lesson on each of the first 36 parshiot of the TORAH (a standard school year). This TORAH-TOONS book contains worksheets and exercises to go with each of these segments. They include a portion of the biblical text (which is the focus), a selection of rabbinic commentary, and some kind of open-ended exercise. In going through this material, you will (1) learn something about the process of Jewish Torah Study, (2) come to understand the style of serval of the major commentators, and (3) cover a large number of related Jewish topics.

This book, while it can be used independant text, has been designed to used in conjunction with TORAH-TOONS media. There is a detailed teacher's guide, and a set of TORAH-TOONS GAMING PACS. In addition, there is a program called THE MAZE, THE THORN FOREST, THE BOILING POT AND THE WELL - which services as an introduction to the process of biblical commentary. Using these resources may enhance your teaching process.

Enjoy TORAH-TOONS and have fun teaching with it.

JANE GOLUB JOEL LURIE GRISHAVER ALAN ROWE

Special thanks to Dr. Stuart Kelman and Joyce Seglin for their imput, proof-reading and advice.

TORAH-TOONS stars the biblical text and its characters. It also stars the following biblical commentators.

ABRAVANEL: 1437-1508 A Spanish-Jewish commentator, philosopher and statesman. He was born in Lisbon and left Spain in 1492 during the Inquisition. He died in Venice.

ISAAC ARAMA 1420-1494 A Spanish commentator and Talmudicist. He was known as the AKEDAT YITZCHAK. Much of his work was philosophic.

BECHOR SHOR 12th Century A French Talmudicist of the Tosafist school. (The Tosafot were students of Rashi). Only fragments of his works have been published and much of it is still in manuscript.

UMBERTO CASSUTTO 1883-1951 An Italian Bible commentator who moved to Israel in 1939.

HIZKUNI 13th Century. We don't know much about him, though he was probably a student of RASHI.

IBN EZRA 1089-1164 A Spanish Bible commentator, astronomer, poet and grammarian. He traveled extensively, and visited England, France, and North Africa.

BENNO JACOB 1862-1955 A German Bible scholar who fused modern scientific bible study tools with traditional materials.

NEHAMA LEIBOWITZ Contemporary Israeli Bible scholar. She was born in Germany, worked in England during World War II and then made Aliyah. She almost single-handedly helped to popularize study of parshat ha-shavua.

MALBIM = Meir Yehuda Leibush ben Yehiel Michal 1809-1880. Russian rabbi whose commentary on the Torah tries to defend the traditional view of the text.

RAMBAM = Rabbi Moshe ben Maimon (a.k.a. Maimonides) 1135-1204 He was born in Spain and died in Egypt. He was a philosopher, doctor, Bible Scholar and legal expert. Among his books are the Mishneh Torah and The Guide to the Perplexed. He was one of the greatest Jewish minds of all times.

RAMBAN = Rabbi Moshe ben Nachman (a.k.a. Nachmonides) 1194-1270 He was another Spanish Jewish commentator who not only produced works on the Bible and Talmud but was famous for his public debates with the Jewish convert to Christianity - Pablo Christiano in Barcelona in 1263.

RASHBAM = Rabbi Shemuel ben Meir 1080-1158. A French bible scholar who was one of the Tosafot. He was the grandson of RASHI.

RASHI = Rabbi Shlomo Yitzchaki 1040-1105 RASHI is the Jewish Bible commentator. He lived in the Champagne region of France, and earned his living by running a vineyard. His works are the basic reference Jews use for studying both the Torah and the Talmud. What makes his commentaries so special is his style which not only makes the process of the text clear to all who use his commentary (making it possible for a person to teach him/her self), but that his commentary serves as a gateway to all the resources of the Jewish tradition.

Also appearing in TORAH-TOONS are:

Josephus - A famous Jewish Historian
Amos - A prophet
Isaiah - Another prophet
Shakespeare - The famous playwrite
Joel Lurie Grishaver - Your favorite Jewish Cartoonist
and various Talmudic rabbis.

SPECIAL APPEARANCES ARE MADE BY THESE RABBINIC TEXTS

Pirke Avot - Ethics of the Father (A portion of Mishneh)
Selections from the Talmud
Shulchan Aruch - A famous Jewish Law Code
The writings of the Chafetz Chaim

AND SELECTIONS FROM THESE COLLECTIONS OF MIDRASH:

Midrash Rabbah (Genesis Rabbah, Exodus Rabbah, etc.)
Midrash Chemdat Hayamin
Midrash Socher Tov
Midrash Torat Or
Sifrei
Tanchuma
Mekhilta

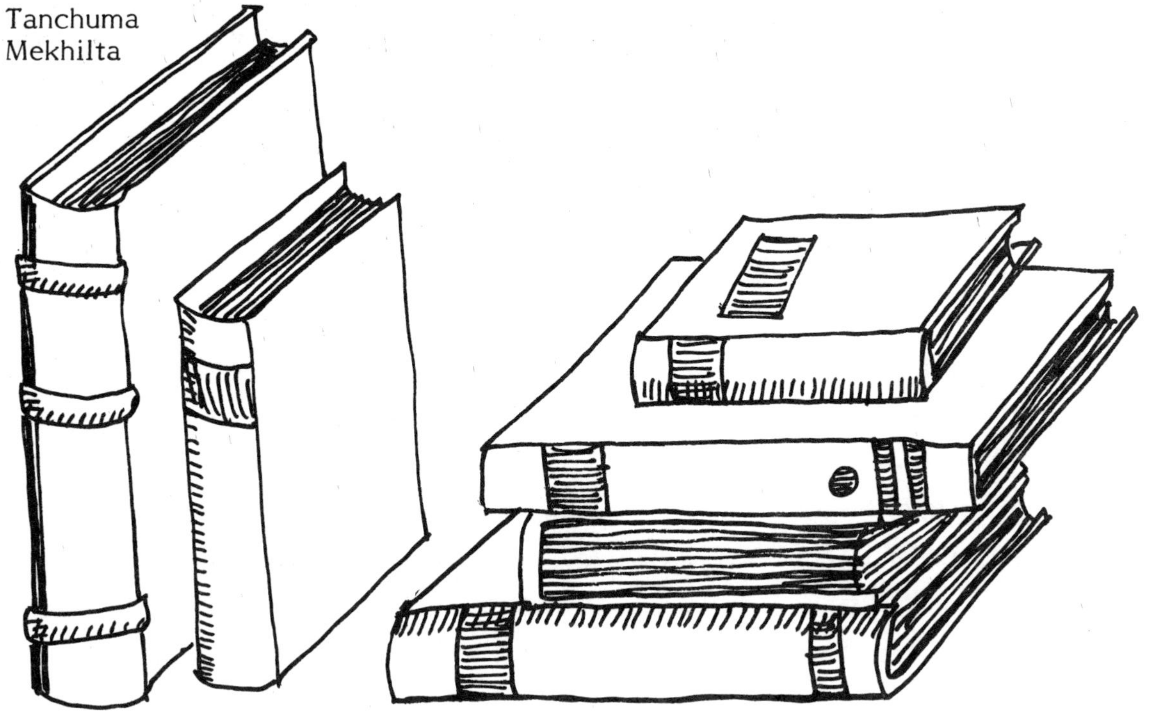

TABLE OF CONTENTS

EPISODE # 1 BEGINNINGS

GEN 1: 1-5

בְּרֵאשִׁית בָּרָא אֱלֹהִים אֵת הַשָּׁמַיִם וְאֵת הָאָרֶץ׃ 2 וְהָאָרֶץ
הָיְתָה תֹהוּ וָבֹהוּ וְחֹשֶׁךְ עַל־פְּנֵי תְהוֹם וְרוּחַ אֱלֹהִים מְרַחֶפֶת עַל־פְּנֵי
הַמָּיִם׃ 3 וַיֹּאמֶר אֱלֹהִים יְהִי אוֹר וַיְהִי־אוֹר׃ 4 וַיַּרְא אֱלֹהִים אֶת־הָאוֹר
כִּי־טוֹב וַיַּבְדֵּל אֱלֹהִים בֵּין הָאוֹר וּבֵין הַחֹשֶׁךְ׃ 5 וַיִּקְרָא אֱלֹהִים ׀ לָאוֹר
יוֹם וְלַחֹשֶׁךְ קָרָא לָיְלָה וַיְהִי־עֶרֶב וַיְהִי־בֹקֶר יוֹם אֶחָד׃

COMPARE THESE TWO TRANSLATIONS. WHAT MAKES THEM SO DIFFERENT?

J.P.S. - 1962	J.P.S. - 1917
When God began to create the heavens and the earth (the earth being unformed and void, with darkness over the surface of the deep and a wind from God sweeping over the water). And God said: "Let there be light", and there was light. God saw that the light was good, and God separated the light from the darkness. God called the light Day, and the darkness Night. And there was evening and there was morning, a first day.	In the beginning God created the heavens and the earth. Now the earth was unformed and void, and the darkness was upon the face of the deep; and the spirit of God hovered over the face of the waters. And God said: "Let there be light." And God saw the light, that it was good and God divided the light from the darkness. And God called the light Day, and the darkness He called Night. And there was evening, and there was morning, one day.
1. In this translation, what does God create on the first day?	1. In this translation, what does God create on the first day?
2. In this translation, what already exists before God begins creation?	2. In this translation, what already exists before God begins creation?

MIDRASH #1 (GEN. R 1.5)

In real life, when a real king builds a palace on a site of sewers, dunghills and garbage - if one says - "The king's palace is built on top of sewers, dunghills and garbage," - doesn't that person insult the king? In the same way, whoever says that this world was created out of tohu and vohu and darkness - doesn't that person insult God's glory.

Rav

Said Rav Huna in Bar Kappara's name:
If the concept (that God created the world out of tohu and vohu) wasn't written in the Torah - it would be impossible to say.

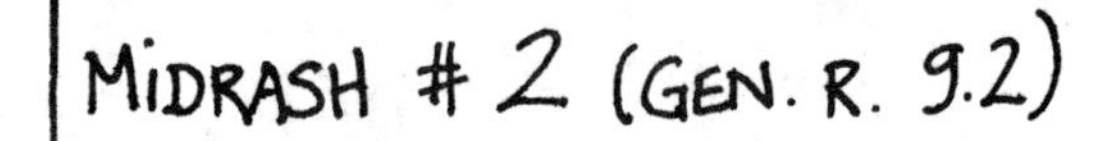

Rabbi Abbahu said:

...the Holy One, blessed be He, kept creating worlds and destroying them, until He created these worlds of heaven and earth. Then he said: "These please me; those did not please me."

1. Does Rabbi Abbahu think that anything existed before Bereshit?

2. Does Rav Huna (in Bar Kappara's name) think that anything existed before Bereshit? Is he comfortable with the idea?

3. What do you think that Rav really thinks about creation?

4. Why doesn't he say that something existed before Bereshit?

5. Can God make a rock so big that God can't move it?

ORDER AND CHAOS

1. Write your own definition of "chaos."

2. Write your own definition of "order." (Think of how hard it is to explain what order really means)

3. List three things in your life which are closer to "chaos" than "order"
   a.
   b.
   c.

4. List three things in your life which are more in "order" than in "chaos".
   a.
   b.
   c.

5. What is the most ordered thing you know?

6. What is the most chaotic thing you know?

7. Do you think that the world is closer to being ordered or being chaotic?

8. Are people responsible for the order or the chaos? Is God responsible for the order or the chaos?

9 אֵלֶּה תּוֹלְדֹת נֹחַ נֹחַ אִישׁ צַדִּיק תָּמִים הָיָה בְּדֹרֹתָיו אֶת־הָאֱלֹהִים
הִתְהַלֶּךְ־נֹחַ׃ 10 וַיּוֹלֶד נֹחַ שְׁלֹשָׁה בָנִים אֶת־שֵׁם אֶת־חָם וְאֶת־יָפֶת׃
11 וַתִּשָּׁחֵת הָאָרֶץ לִפְנֵי הָאֱלֹהִים וַתִּמָּלֵא הָאָרֶץ חָמָס׃ 12 וַיַּרְא אֱלֹהִים
אֶת־הָאָרֶץ וְהִנֵּה נִשְׁחָתָה כִּי־הִשְׁחִית כָּל־בָּשָׂר אֶת־דַּרְכּוֹ עַל־
הָאָרֶץ׃

These are the generations of No-ach
No-ach was a righteous man, whole-hearted - "in his generation"
No-ach walked with God.
And No-ach fathered three sons: Shem, Ham and Yaphet.
And the earth was corrupt before God - and the earth was filled with violence.
And God saw the earth, and behold it was corrupt-
for all living things had corrupted their ways upon the earth.

1. What is the problem with the phrase "in his generation?" What two things could it mean?

a. ______________________________

b. ______________________________

2. Which do you think it means? Why?

____

____

____

COMPARING NO·ACH AND AV·RAHAM

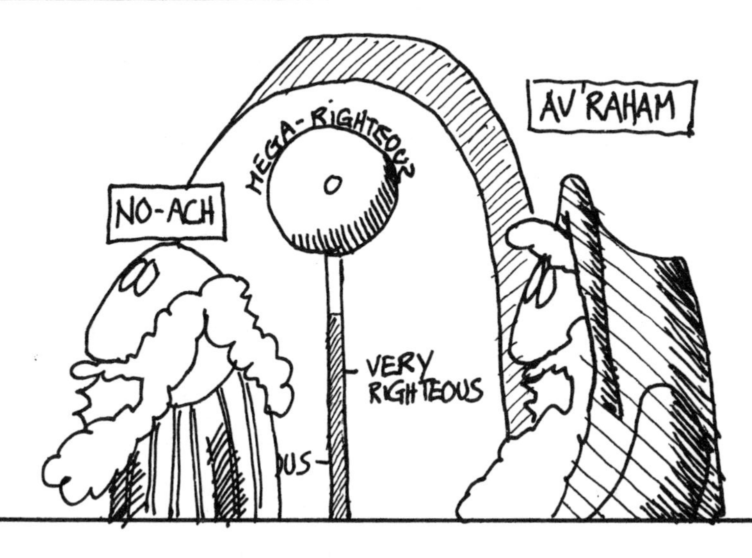

Genesis 6:9	No-ach was a righteous man, whole -hearted in his generation.
Genesis 18:18ff	Av-raham is to be a great and populous nation, and all the nations of the earth are to be blessed through him. For I have singled him out...to keep the way of the Lord by doing what is just and right...
Job 1:1	There was a man in the land of Uz, whose name is Job; and that man was whole-hearted and upright, and one that feared God and shunned evil.

1. Why is it logical to compare No-ach and Av-raham in regard to their righteousness?

____

____

____

2. List as many things as you can which No-ach and Av-raham have in common.

______________ ______________

______________ ______________

______________ ______________

Some of our rabbis explain "In his generation" to his credit: meaning - he was righteous even in his generation - it follows that had he lived in a generation of righteous people he would have been ever more righteous.

Other rabbis explain it to his discredit. In his own generation he was considered righteous, but if he had lived in a generation of righteous people, for example in the generation of Av-raham, he would not have been outstanding.

Rashi on Genesis 6:9

CONTINUED

1. What two explanations of "in his generation" does Rashi bring down from the midrash?

a. ______________________________

b. ______________________________

2. Why does Rashi bring down both midrashim?

____

____

3. Do we know which midrash Rashi believes?

____

____

Genesis 9:6 No-ach walks with God.

Genesis 24:40 The Lord before whom I (Av-raham) walk.

3. What can you learn by comparing these two verses?

____

____

____

RASHI'S COMMENT

No-ach needed God's support to hold him up in his righteousness, while Av-raham drew his strength from himself, and walked in his righteousness.

4. How does Rashi use the two verses to compare No-ach and Av-raham?

____

____

____

5. Does Rashi let us know what he thinks about the meaning of "in his generation?" (What? and How?)

____

____

____

THOUGHT QUESTION

Is it easy or hard to be righteous in our generation?

____

____

EPISODE # 3 - THE GOING

GEN. 11.27-12.1

These are the generations of Terach
Terach fathered Av-ram, Nachor and Haran
and Haran fathered Lot.
Haran died before Terach his father in the land of his birth
in Ur of the Chaldeans
Av-ram married and Nachor married
The name of Av-ram's wife was Sarai
The name of Nachor's wife was Milka...
Now Sarai was barren - she had no child.

Terach took Av-ram his son and Lot son of Haran - his son's son
and Sarai his daughter-in-law, his son Av-ram's wife
They went out together from Ur of Chaldeans to go to the land of Canaan.
And the days of Terach were two-hundred and five.
Terach died in Haran.

END OF PAR-SHAT NO-ACH

אוַיֹּאמֶר יְהוָה אֶל־אַבְרָם
לֶךְ־לְךָ מֵאַרְצְךָ וּמִמּוֹלַדְתְּךָ וּמִבֵּית אָבִיךָ אֶל־הָאָרֶץ אֲשֶׁר אַרְאֶךָּ׃

BEGINNING OF LECH LECHA

The Lord said to Av-ram
Go you forth
from your land
from your birth place
from your father's house
to the land which I will show you.

1. Why does the family leave Ur?

____

____

2. Why does the family stop in Haran?

____

____

3. Why does Av-ram listen to God and immediately follow the instructions to leave without any questions?

____

____

MIDRASH # 2

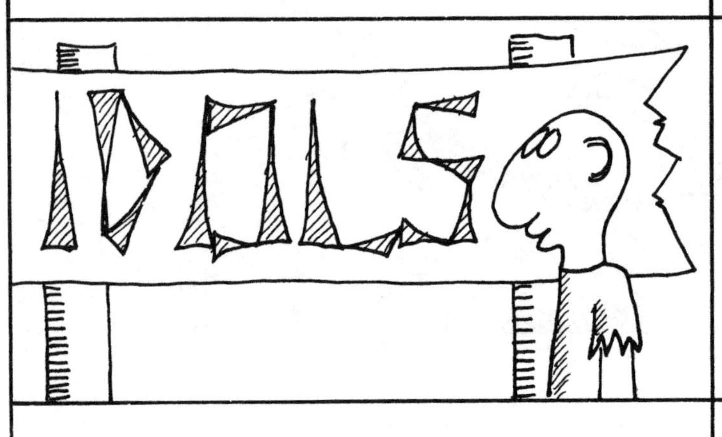

Av-ram's father Terach made and sold idols for a living. He had an idol shop. One day he left Av-ram in charge of the idol shop. A man came into the shop and asked to buy an idol from the shelf. He asked the man "How old are you?" The man answered, "I am fifty." Av-ram then asked the man, "Do you really expect protection from an idol my father carved last week?" The man left the shop.

Next an old woman came into the idol shop. She said, "My house was broken into and robbed. Among other things, they stole my god. I want to buy another god. Av-ram said to her, "Your last idol could not protect your home, now you want to buy a new house-god. Do you think this idol will protect your home better than the last one?"

The old woman left the store angrily. When Terach heard about it, he wasn't very happy about it either.

1. Where in the biblical text is this midrash meant to fit?

   ____

   ____

2. What questions about the biblical text does this midrash answer?

   ____

   ____

   ____

CONTINUED

MIDRASH # 3

One day Av-ram brought a plate of food into the idol shop. He placed it in the middle of the room full of idols. He took a stick and broke all but the largest of the idols. He placed the stick in the largest idol's hand.

When Terach returned to his shop and saw the mess, he asked his son, "Who did this?" Av-ram answered: "The idols were hungry and I brought them food. They all began to fight over the food. A big idol took the stick and killed the other idols."

His father said to him, "You are lying to me! You know that idols cannot talk or move or do any kind of action." Av-ram said to his father, "Listen to your own words."

Terach came to accept his son's belief that there was only one God. People in Ur didn't like Av-ram and Terach attacking their religion. After a few things happened, Terach and family decided to leave Ur of the Chaldeans. (Why they left Haran is another Midrash).

1. Where in the biblical text is this midrash meant to fit?

   ____

   ____

2. What questions about the biblical text does this midrash answer?

   ____

   ____

   ____

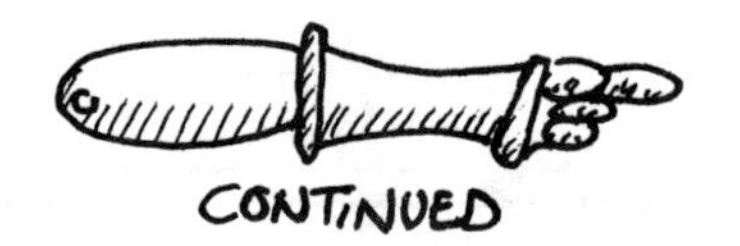

3. What is the "message" of this midrash?

3. What is the "message" of this midrash?

MIDRASH # 1

When Av-ram was a boy, his parents had to hide him because an evil king named Nimrod wanted to kill him (the story of why is another midrash). To keep Av-ram safe, he was hidden in a cave which was high on a mountainside.

One night, Av-ram came out of his cave and saw the moon and stars. He thought: "The moon and stars must be gods, because they are so beautiful and because they rule the night...." Av-ram began to pray to the moon and stars, but morning came and they disappeared.

The sun rose, giving warmth and light. Av-ram thought that the sun must be a god. So he began to pray to the sun. Soon, up came a wind and blew some clouds in front of the sun. It cut off the light and warmth. Rather than thinking that the wind and clouds were gods - Av-ram finally had an insight.

The idea hit him like a flash. "There must be one God who controls everything: sun, moon, stars, wind, clouds, rain - everything." He said, "That God alone will I worship." It was then that Av-ram heard a voice: "I am here my son."

1. What questions about the biblical text does this midrash answer?

2. What does this midrash teach us about Av-ram?

THOUGHT QUESTION

Have you ever felt close to God?

EPISODE # 4 THE BARGAIN

GEN. 18:17-21

17 וַיהוָה אָמָר הַמְכַסֶּה אֲנִי מֵאַבְרָהָם
אֲשֶׁר אֲנִי עֹשֶׂה׃ 18 וְאַבְרָהָם הָיוֹ יִהְיֶה לְגוֹי גָּדוֹל וְעָצוּם וְנִבְרְכוּ בוֹ
כֹּל גּוֹיֵי הָאָרֶץ׃ 19 כִּי יְדַעְתִּיו לְמַעַן אֲשֶׁר יְצַוֶּה אֶת־בָּנָיו וְאֶת־בֵּיתוֹ
אַחֲרָיו וְשָׁמְרוּ דֶּרֶךְ יְהוָה לַעֲשׂוֹת צְדָקָה וּמִשְׁפָּט לְמַעַן הָבִיא יְהוָה
עַל־אַבְרָהָם אֵת אֲשֶׁר־דִּבֶּר עָלָיו׃ 20 וַיֹּאמֶר יְהוָה זַעֲקַת סְדֹם וַעֲמֹרָה
כִּי־רָבָּה וְחַטָּאתָם כִּי כָבְדָה מְאֹד׃ 21 אֵרְדָה־נָּא וְאֶרְאֶה הַכְּצַעֲקָתָהּ
הַבָּאָה אֵלַי עָשׂוּ ׀ כָּלָה וְאִם־לֹא אֵדָעָה׃

Now the Lord had said:

Shall I hide from Av-raham that which I am about to do -
since Av-raham is to become a great and populous nation
and through him will all the nations of the earth be blessed.

Fo I have singled him out, that he may instruct his children and his offspring
to keep the way of the Lord by doing what is just and right -
in order that the Lord may bring about for Av-raham - that which He has promised.

Then the Lord said, "The outcry against Sodom and Gomorra - indeed it increases and
their sin indeed weighs very heavily.
I will go down to see if they have acted according to the outcry which has come to Me,
If not - I will know it.

1. This passage is made up of three verses.

   a. The first verse is God explaining ______________________.

   b. The third verse is God telling ______________________.

What is the second verse?

____

____

____

2. How do you understand God's reasons for telling Av-ram?

____

____

Here are three explanations of why God chose to inform Av-raham about Sodom:

AMOS · 750 BCE

For the Lord will not do anything until he has revealed His counsel to his servants, the prophets.

What connects this statement of Amos to Av-raham? (Clue - Genesis 20:7)

____

____

____

____

RASHI · 1075

SHALL I HIDE - God is asking a question. "It is not right for Me to do this without his knowing because I gave him this land and these five cities are his.

I called him Av-raham - meaning the father of a multitude of nations - should I destroy the children without informing the father who loves Me?"

In this commentary, whose voice is speaking?

____

____

Can you find the places in the text which support Rashi's interpretation?

____

____

CASSUTO · 1930

God tested Av-raham ten times : 1) Having to leave Haran; 2) Having to go to Egpyt; 3) Having to split up with Lot; 4) Having to rescue Lot; 5) Having Hagar (not Sara) give birth; 6) Having the mitzvah of circumcision; 7) Having to argue over Sodom; 8) Having to go down to Avimelech; 9) Having to exile Ishmael; 10) Having the binding of Isaac.

Can you find something in the text which leads you to believe that this was a test?

____

List the 10 most difficult trials you've had to go through.

1. ____________________ 6. ____________________
2. ____________________ 7. ____________________
3. ____________________ 8. ____________________
4. ____________________ 9. ____________________
5. ____________________ 10. ____________________

Compare these two lists of the 10 tests Av-raham faced.

CASSUTO

1. Leaving Haran (12:1)
2. Going to Egypt (12:10)
3. Split with Lot (13:5)
4. Rescuing Lot (15:1)
5. Ishmael's birth (16)
6. Circumcision (17)
7. Sodom (18:17)
8. Going to Abimelech (20:1)
9. Exiling Ishmael (21:8)
10. Binding of Isaac (22:1)

PIRKE AVOT (via Avot D'Rabbi Natan 33)

1. Twice ordered to move:
   a. Genesis 12:1
   b. Genesis 12:10
2. Twice with his sons:
   a. Genesis 21:10
   b. Genesis 22:1
3. Twice with his wives
   a. Genesis 12:11
   b. Genesis 21:10
4. War with Kings (14:13)
5. Covenant between the pieces (15)
6. Once in Ur (by Nimrod)
7. At circumcision (17:19)

A. Compare the two lists - what are the differences?

____

____

B. How do you think Cassuto arrived at his list?

____

C. How do you think the rabbis arrived at the list in Avot D'Rabbi Natan?

____

D. What sources did Cassuto use?

____

E. What sources did rabbis use?

____

F. Did they read the Torah differently?

____

____

G. What do you think is important about there being "10 Trials" (regardless of the different lists)?

____

____

1 וַיִּהְיוּ חַיֵּי שָׂרָה מֵאָה שָׁנָה וְעֶשְׂרִים שָׁנָה וְשֶׁבַע שָׁנִים שְׁנֵי
חַיֵּי שָׂרָה׃ 2 וַתָּמָת שָׂרָה בְּקִרְיַת אַרְבַּע הִוא חֶבְרוֹן בְּאֶרֶץ כְּנָעַן
וַיָּבֹא אַבְרָהָם לִסְפֹּד לְשָׂרָה וְלִבְכֹּתָהּ׃ 3 וַיָּקָם אַבְרָהָם מֵעַל פְּנֵי
מֵתוֹ וַיְדַבֵּר אֶל־בְּנֵי־חֵת לֵאמֹר׃ 4 גֵּר־וְתוֹשָׁב אָנֹכִי עִמָּכֶם תְּנוּ לִי
אֲחֻזַּת־קֶבֶר עִמָּכֶם וְאֶקְבְּרָה מֵתִי מִלְּפָנָי׃ 5 וַיַּעֲנוּ בְנֵי־חֵת אֶת־אַבְרָהָם
לֵאמֹר לוֹ׃ 6 שְׁמָעֵנוּ ׀ אֲדֹנִי נְשִׂיא אֱלֹהִים אַתָּה בְּתוֹכֵנוּ בְּמִבְחַר
קְבָרֵינוּ קְבֹר אֶת־מֵתֶךָ אִישׁ מִמֶּנּוּ אֶת־קִבְרוֹ לֹא־יִכְלֶה מִמְּךָ מִקְּבֹר
מֵתֶךָ׃

Sara's lifetime - the span of Sara's life came to one hundred and twenty-seven years.
Sara died in Kiriat-Arba - now called Hevron - in the land of Canaan.
And Av-raham mourned for Sara and bewailed her.
Then Av-raham rose from the face of his dead and spoke to the Hittites saying:

> I am a stranger and a settler with you.
> Sell me a burial site among you -
> that I may bury my dead from before my face.

And the sons of Het replied to Av-raham saying to him:

> Hear us my Lord,
> You are a prince of God among us.
> Bury your dead in the choicest of our burial places;
> none of us will withhold his burial place from you
> to bury your dead.

Av-raham rose and bowed before the people of the land - before the sons of Het, and he spoke with them saying:

> If it is your wish that I remove my dead from before my face
> you must agree to intercede for me with Ephron son of Zohar.
> Let him sell me the cave of Machpela which belongs to him -
> which is at the edge of his land.
> Let him sell it to me at its full worth in silver - for a burial site in your midst.

Ephron was present among the Hittites; so Ephron the Hittite answered Av-raham in the hearing of the sons of Het - all who entered into the council gates of the city saying:

CONTINUED

No, my lord, hear me!
I give you the field and I give you the cave which is in it.
Before the eyes of the sons of Het my people - I give it to you.
Bury your dead.

Then Av-raham bowed low before the people of the land
and spoke to Ephron in the hearing of the people of the land - saying:

But if you yourself would only hear me!
I will give the silver-worth of the land
Take it from me - so that I may bury my dead there.

Ephron answered Av-raham saying to him:

My lord, hear me!
A piece of land worth four hundred silver-weight - What is it between us?
Bury your dead!

Av-raham listened to Ephron. Av-raham weighed out to Ephron the money that he had named out in the hearing of the Sons of Het - four hundred shekels of silver at the going merchant's rate. So Ephron's land in Machpela, near Mamre - the field with its cave and all the trees within its confines - passed to Av-raham as his possession - before the eyes of the Sons of Het and all who had entered into the council gates.

THE MALBIM: What contribution does such a story make to the spiritual message and mission of the Torah?

____

____

____

Look at the speeches made in this story - decide which are honest, which are dishonest, and which are polite-formal ritual statements.

Avraham - I am a stranger...____________________

Sons of Het - Hear us my Lord...____________________

Avraham - If it is your wish...____________________

Ephron - No my lord, hear me!____________________

Avraham - But if you yourself would only hear me...____________________

Ephron - My lord, hear me!____________________

Put each of these speeches in your own words:

Avraham - I am a stranger...____________________

Sons of Het - Hear us my lord...____________________

Avraham - If it is your wish...____________________

Ephron - No my lord, hear me!____________________

Avraham - But if you yourself would only hear me...____________________

____

Ephron - My lord, hear me!____________________

Look at each of these explanations of the reason the Torah tells this story.

a. Find what in the story supports each explanation.

b. Decide which of these explanations you accept.

RABBI YUDAN BAR SIMON

This is one of three places about which the nations of the world cannot complain saying: "These are stolen lands." These places are the Cave of Machpela, the Temple and the burial place of Joseph. All of these places were purchased. (See Gen. 23:16, 1 Chron 21:25 and Gen. 33:19)

What is the story which supports this explanation?

____

____

____

RAMBAM

This chapter was written in order to show the lovingkindness of God towards Av-raham. He became a prince in a land to which he had come as a stranger. Though he had never told anyone that he was a prince or a great man - they nevertheless addressed him by the title "my lord."

What in the story supports this explanation?

____

____

____

HIZKUNI

And Av-raham rose up and bowed down to the people of the land .. Av-raham needed all of them. Though Ephron had sold him the field, Av-raham was not authorized to use it as a burial ground without permission of his fellow citizens.

What in the story supports this explanation?

____

____

____

EPISODE # 6 THE STRUGGLE

[21] וַיֶּעְתַּר יִצְחָק
לַיהוָה לְנֹכַח אִשְׁתּוֹ כִּי עֲקָרָה הִוא וַיֵּעָתֶר לוֹ יְהוָה וַתַּהַר רִבְקָה
אִשְׁתּוֹ׃ [22] וַיִּתְרֹצְצוּ הַבָּנִים בְּקִרְבָּהּ וַתֹּאמֶר אִם־כֵּן לָמָּה זֶּה אָנֹכִי
וַתֵּלֶךְ לִדְרֹשׁ אֶת־יְהוָה׃ [23] וַיֹּאמֶר יְהוָה לָהּ
שְׁנֵי גֹייִם בְּבִטְנֵךְ וּשְׁנֵי לְאֻמִּים מִמֵּעַיִךְ יִפָּרֵדוּ
וּלְאֹם מִלְאֹם יֶאֱמָץ וְרַב יַעֲבֹד צָעִיר׃

Yitzchak entreated the Lord for his wife - for she was barren.
And the Lord allowed Himself to be entreated.
Rivka his wife became pregnant.
But the children struggled in her womb
and she said:
If this is so, why am I?
She went to inquire of the Lord
and the Lord answered her:
Two nations are in your womb,
Two separate peoples shall issue from your body;
One people shall be mightier than the other,
and the older shall serve the younger.

Do you think that the pain Rivka was feeling was "normal" or do you think something exceptional was happening?

____

____

____

What evidence can you find in the text for your opinion?

____

____

____

RASHI'S COMMENT

AND THE CHILDREN STRUGGLED...

You must admit that this verse demands a midrashic explanation - since it gives no explanation as to why the struggling is happening. The text says that she exclaimed: "If this is so, why am I?" It seems that she is asking if this was normal.

Our Rabbis explained that the word has the meaning of running, or moving quickly: whenever she passed by the doors of the Torah (meaning the Yeshiva of Shem and Ever) Ya-akov moved quickly in his efforts to be born, but whenever she passed by the gates of a pagen temple, Esau ran to be born. (Genesis R. 63)

Another explanation is: They struggled with one another and quarreled as to how they should divide the two worlds (this world and the world to come) as their inheritance.

AND SHE SAID, IF the pain of pregnancy is SO great, WHY did I long and pray so hard to become pregnant. (Gen R 63)

1. Why does Rashi feel that this verse needs a midrash to explain it?

____

____

2. List the explanations Rashi gives for the struggling?

   a. ______________________________

   b. ______________________________

   c. ______________________________

3. Why do you think Rashi brings you more than one explanation?

____

____

____

THOUGHT QUESTION

What is the biggest struggle going on inside of you?

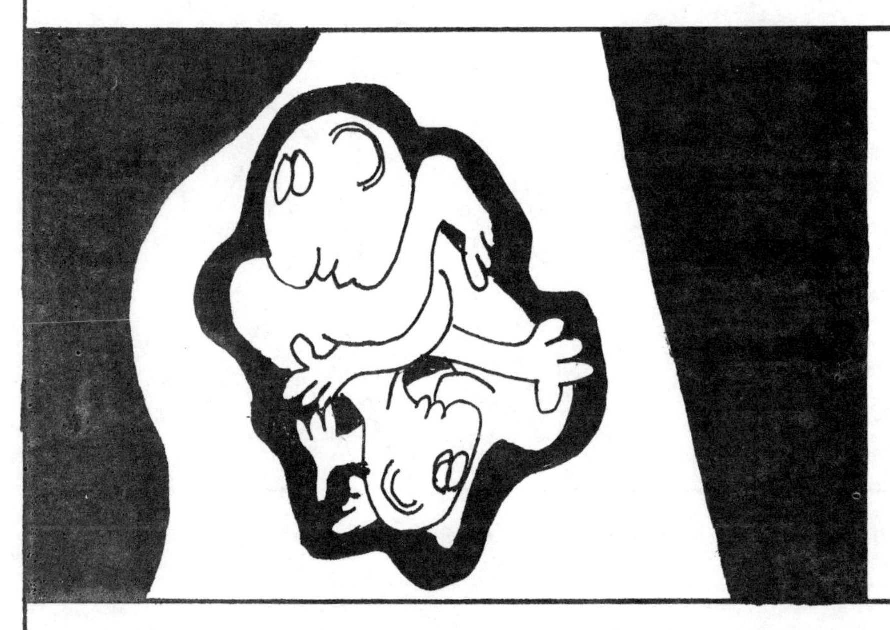

"אִם-כֵּן לָמָה
זֶה אָנֹכִי?"

"IF THIS IS SO - WHY AM I?"

When have you wanted to say - "If this is so - why am I?"

THOUGHT QUESTION

EPISODE # 7: UPS AND DOWNS

GEN. 28: 11-13

יַעֲקֹב מִבְּאֵר שָׁבַע וַיֵּלֶךְ חָרָנָה׃ 11 וַיִּפְגַּע בַּמָּקוֹם וַיָּלֶן שָׁם כִּי־בָא
הַשֶּׁמֶשׁ וַיִּקַּח מֵאַבְנֵי הַמָּקוֹם וַיָּשֶׂם מְרַאֲשֹׁתָיו וַיִּשְׁכַּב בַּמָּקוֹם הַהוּא׃
12 וַיַּחֲלֹם וְהִנֵּה סֻלָּם מֻצָּב אַרְצָה וְרֹאשׁוֹ מַגִּיעַ הַשָּׁמָיְמָה וְהִנֵּה מַלְאֲכֵי
אֱלֹהִים עֹלִים וְיֹרְדִים בּוֹ׃ 13 וְהִנֵּה יְהוָה נִצָּב עָלָיו וַיֹּאמַר אֲנִי יְהוָה
אֱלֹהֵי אַבְרָהָם אָבִיךָ וֵאלֹהֵי יִצְחָק הָאָרֶץ אֲשֶׁר אַתָּה שֹׁכֵב עָלֶיהָ
לְךָ אֶתְּנֶנָּה וּלְזַרְעֶךָ׃

Ya-akov left Beer-Sheva and went toward Haran.
He came upon that place and had to spend the night there
for the sun had come in.
He took one of the stones of that place
and he dreamt:
Here, a ladder was set up on the earth
and its head touching heaven.
Here, angels of God going up and down on it.
Here the Lord was standing beside him and said:
I am the Lord, the God of your father Av-raham and the God of Yitzchak
The land on which you lie
I give it to you and to your seed.

1. Look carefully at Ya-akov's dream. What seems wrong?

 ____

 ____

2. What promise is made to Ya-akov? Does it seem familiar?

 ____

 ____

MIDRASH #1 (VIA RASHI)	MIDRASH #2 (PESIKTA D'RAV KAHANA)
 ISRAEL NOT ISRAEL	
The angels that escorted him within the Holy Land do not go outside the Holy Land. They therefore ascended to Heaven. The angels which were to escort him outside the Holy Land descended to go with him.	This text teaches that the Holy One, Blessed Be He, showed Ya-akov the angel of Babylon ascending and descending - then that of Media, then Greece, then Rome. Said the Holy One Blessed Be He to Ya-akov: "Ya-akov, why don't you ascend - If you ascend, you shall suffer no descent. But he did not believe Him and did not ascend.
1. How does this Midrash solve our problem? __________ __________ __________	1. How does this Midrash solve our problem? __________ __________ __________
2. What is the message of this Midrash? __________ __________ __________	2. What is the message of this Midrash? __________ __________ __________

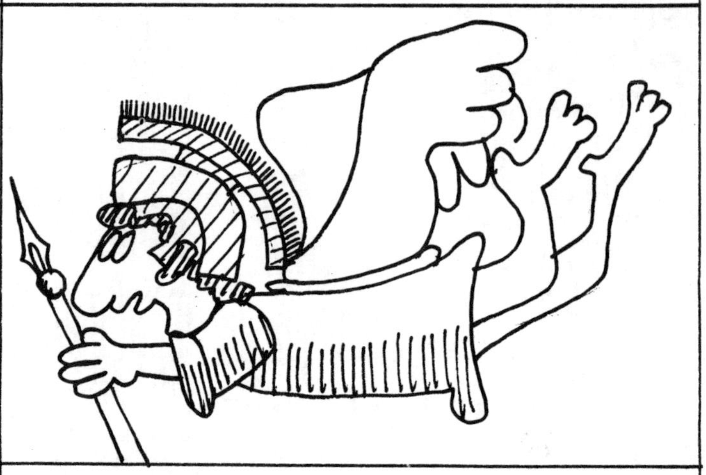

THOUGHT QUESTION

What things in your life cause you to go up and down?

____

____

____

____

____

____

____

EPISODE # 8 - THE GATHERING GEN. 32. 25-29

[25] וַיִּוָּתֵר יַעֲקֹב לְבַדּוֹ וַיֵּאָבֵק אִישׁ עִמּוֹ עַד
עֲלוֹת הַשָּׁחַר׃ [26] וַיַּרְא כִּי לֹא יָכֹל לוֹ וַיִּגַּע בְּכַף־יְרֵכוֹ וַתֵּקַע כַּף־יֶרֶךְ
יַעֲקֹב בְּהֵאָבְקוֹ עִמּוֹ׃ [27] וַיֹּאמֶר שַׁלְּחֵנִי כִּי עָלָה הַשָּׁחַר וַיֹּאמֶר לֹא
אֲשַׁלֵּחֲךָ כִּי אִם־בֵּרַכְתָּנִי׃ [28] וַיֹּאמֶר אֵלָיו מַה־שְּׁמֶךָ וַיֹּאמֶר יַעֲקֹב׃
[29] וַיֹּאמֶר לֹא יַעֲקֹב יֵאָמֵר עוֹד שִׁמְךָ כִּי אִם־יִשְׂרָאֵל כִּי־שָׂרִיתָ עִם־
אֱלֹהִים וְעִם־אֲנָשִׁים וַתּוּכָל׃

Ya-akov was left alone -
A man wrestled with him until dawn arose.
When he saw that he could not win against him
he touched the socket of his hip
and the socket of Ya-akov's hip was strained as he wrestled with him.
Then he said: "Let me go for the dawn is rising."
But he said: "I will not let you go unless you bless me."
Then he said to him: "What is your name?"
And he said: "Ya-akov."
Then he said: "No longer will your name be Ya-akov, the heel
rather Yisrael, the God wrestler,
for you have struggled with God and with people and won."

1. What do you think the name change means?

___

___

___

2. Compare it to other name changes in the Bible.

___

___

___

CONTINUED

GEN. 35:9-11

And God let Himself be seen by Ya-akov again, when he came from the Aramean field,
and He blessed him
and God said to him:
Ya-akov is your name - but no more shall your name be called Ya-akov,
Rather, Yisrael shall be your name.
And he called his name Yisrael.

Looking at these verses, there are a lot of questions to be answered.

1. Why is Ya-akov's name changed twice?

 ____

2. Why does Ya-akov ask his wrestling partner to bless him - wasn't he already blessed when he stole the birthright from Esau?

 ____

3. Why is Ya-akov satisfied with a name change when he asks for a blessing?

 ____

4. Why does God add a blessing when God changes his name?

 ____

Look at Rashi's comments on these verses and see how he answers them.

YOUR NAME NO MORE SHALL BE YA-AKOV

Not Jacob, the heel/thief shall your name be. It shall no longer be that blessings come to you through stealing and cunning - but now through noble conduct - done honestly.

Later the Holy One blessed be He will allow you to see God at Beth El and will change your name. There God will bless you.

In Rashi's comment, who is speaking? ______________________________

How does Rashi answer these questions?

1. Why is Ya-akov's name changed twice?

 ____

 ____

2. Why does Ya-akov ask for a blessing? (Clue: Rashi's comment on Ya-akov's request: Admit that I deserved the blessing which my father gave to me to which Esau lays claim.

 ____

 ____

3. Why is Ya-akov satisfied with a name change and not a blessing?

 ____

 ____

4. Why does God add a blessing while changing Ya-akov's name?

 ____

Compare Yitzchak's blessing of Ya-akov with that which God gives him:

GEN. 27.28-9	GEN. 35.11-12

My God give you the dew of heavens and from the fat of the earth much grain and new wine. People will serve you masses will bow to you You will rule over your brothers your mother's son will bow to you. Those who curse you will be cursed. Those who bless you will be blessed.	Be fruitful and multiply. A nation - groups of nations shall be from you kings shall come from your loins The land which I gave to Avraham and to Yitzchak I give to you and to your seed after you.

1. What do the two blessings have in common?

____

____

2. What is only in Yitzchak's blessing?

____

____

3. What is only in God's blessing?

____

____

4. How does Yitzchak's blessing fit Ya-akov (the heel) and how does God's blessing fit Yisrael (the God wrestler)?

____

____

____

LET'S PLAY WITH NAMES.

YOUR NAME:____

WHO WERE YOU NAMED AFTER?____________________________

WHAT WAS SHE/HE/THEY LIKE?___________________________

____

HOW DID YOUR PARENTS WANT YOU TO BE LIKE THEM?__________

____

HOW ARE YOU LIKE THEM?_______________________________

____

____

What were these Biblical Characters like after their names were changed?

AV'RAM	Avram was a wandering prince. God told him that his descendants would inherit the land of Canaan. The only problem is - Avram has no sons to leave the land he hasn't yet inherited.	God changed Avram's name to Av-ra-ham (father of many nations). At that point_______________
YA'AKOV	Ya-akov was "the heel". He steals the birthright and blessing from his brother, Esau, and then tricks his father-in-law into making him a wealthy man.	God changes Ya-akov's name to Yis-rael "the God wrestler." At that point_______________
HOSHEA	Hoshea was a minor figure. Moses kind of liked him, but nobody really notices him.	Just before he goes on a mission as a spy, Moses changes his name from Hoshea (God helps us) to Ye-ho-shua (God will help us). From that point_______________
YOU	My regular name is__________ and when I am called it I am__________	Another name I am called is__________ and when I am called it, I am__________

EPISODE # 9: THE KIDNAPPING

GEN. 37. 12-14

[12] וַיֵּלְכוּ אֶחָיו לִרְעוֹת אֶת־צֹאן אֲבִיהֶם בִּשְׁכֶם׃ [13] וַיֹּאמֶר יִשְׂרָאֵל אֶל־יוֹסֵף הֲלוֹא אַחֶיךָ רֹעִים בִּשְׁכֶם לְכָה וְאֶשְׁלָחֲךָ אֲלֵיהֶם וַיֹּאמֶר לוֹ הִנֵּנִי׃ [14] וַיֹּאמֶר לוֹ לֶךְ־נָא רְאֵה אֶת־שְׁלוֹם אַחֶיךָ וְאֶת־שְׁלוֹם הַצֹּאן וַהֲשִׁבֵנִי דָּבָר וַיִּשְׁלָחֵהוּ מֵעֵמֶק חֶבְרוֹן וַיָּבֹא שְׁכֶמָה׃

When his brothers had gone to pasture their father's flocks in Shechem, Yisrael said to Yosef: "Your brothers are pasturing in Shechem - come, I will send you to them." He said: "Hineini."

What is unusual about Yosef's answer?

____

____

____

And it came to pass after these things that God tested Avraham and said to him:
Avraham
He said: "Hineini."
He said: "Now take your son, your only son, whom you love, Yitzchak, and go you forth to the land of Moriya and offer him up there for an offering...

And an angel of the Lord appeared to him in a flame of fire out of the bush. And he looked and hinei the bush burned in flame but was not consumed. Moses said, "I will turn aside and look at this great sight - why doesn't the bush burn up?' When the Lord saw that he had turned aside to look, God called to him out of the bush. And He said: "Moses, Moses."
And he said: "Hineini."

CONTINUED

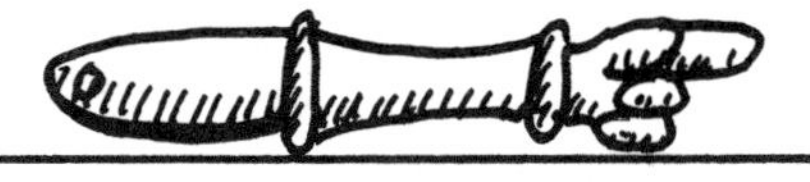

And it came to pass at that time - that Eli was laid down in his place -
his eyes had begun to was dim - so that he could not see -
and the lamp of God had not yet gone out
And Samuel was laid down to sleep in the Temple of the Lord where the ark of God was -
that the Lord called Samuel - and he said: "Hineini."

1. Why is Hineini the right answer for each of these moments?

____

____

____

2. What would you expect people to say at these moments?

____

____

SOME COMMENTS BY RASHI

Look at the way these two comments of Rashi fit together:

1. When God tests Avraham - asking him to sacrifice his son - Avraham answers "HINEINI."
   This is the way Rashi explains the meaning of that answer.

   Genesis 22:1 - HINEINI - that is the answer of a righteous person - expressing meekness and readiness.

What is Rashi trying to explain about Avraham's comment? What does Rashi think the answer HINEINI means? What is Avraham telling God?

____

____

____

When Yosef's father asks him to go to his brothers in the field - Yosef answers "HINEINI."
This is the way Rashi explains the meaning of that answer.

Genesis 37:4 - HINEINI - An expression denoting humility and readiness. he was ready to perform his father's bidding - even though he knew that his brothers hated him.

What is Rashi trying to explain about the meaning of Yosef's comment? What does he think the answer HINEINI means? What is Yosef telling his father?

____

____

CONTINUED

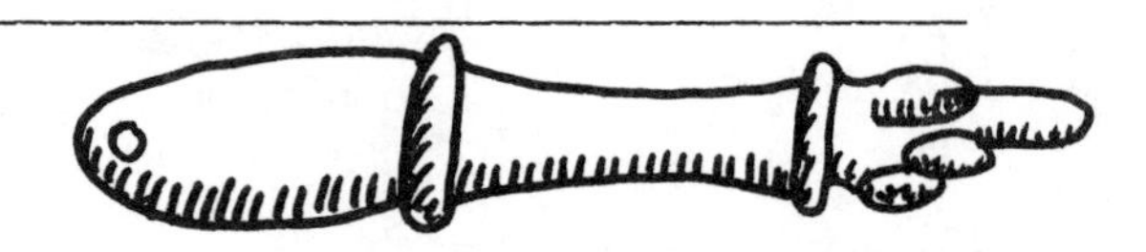

1. What is similar about the two moments?

2. What is similar about the way Avraham and Yosef respond?

THOUGHT SHEET

Even though Avraham, Yosef, Moshe and Samuel all answer HINEINI - they may have had a lot of other things they wanted to say. Fill in some of their thoughts:

AV-RAHAM

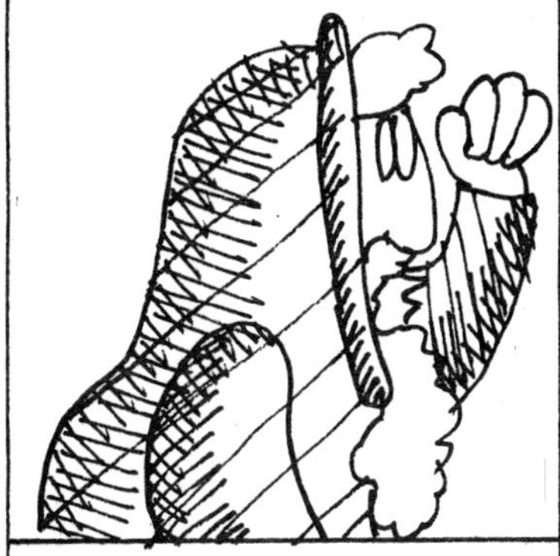

God tells Avraham - "Take Isaac and offer him as a sacrifice on one of the mountain tops which I will show you." Avraham says: "HINEINI." He might have wanted to say:

MOSHE

Moshe is out as a shepherd. He has been through a lot. Being an orphan, committing a murder living in a foreign land. Through all of that - God was silent. Meanwhile his whole people were still enslaved in Egypt. Then, out of nowhere, God talks to him out of a burning bush. Moshe answered: "HINEINI." What else might he have wanted to say?

YOSEF	Yosef is always getting picked on by his brothers. One day his father asks him to go out and visit his brothers in the fields. Yosef answers his father: "HINEINI." He might have wanted to say:
SAMUEL	Samuel was sleeping in the Temple. Three times a voice awakened him in his sleep. He answered: "HINEINI" each time. What else might he have wanted to say?
YOU	I ______________________________. I answered: "HINEINI." Even though I wanted to say:

HINEINI

EPISODE #10 THE RECONCILIATION

GEN. 42:6-9

6 וְיוֹסֵף הוּא הַשַּׁלִּיט עַל־הָאָרֶץ הוּא
הַמַּשְׁבִּיר לְכָל־עַם הָאָרֶץ וַיָּבֹאוּ אֲחֵי יוֹסֵף וַיִּשְׁתַּחֲווּ־לוֹ אַפַּיִם אָרְצָה׃
7 וַיַּרְא יוֹסֵף אֶת־אֶחָיו וַיַּכִּרֵם וַיִּתְנַכֵּר אֲלֵיהֶם וַיְדַבֵּר אִתָּם קָשׁוֹת
וַיֹּאמֶר אֲלֵהֶם מֵאַיִן בָּאתֶם וַיֹּאמְרוּ מֵאֶרֶץ כְּנַעַן לִשְׁבָּר־אֹכֶל׃
8 וַיַּכֵּר יוֹסֵף אֶת־אֶחָיו וְהֵם לֹא הִכִּרֻהוּ׃ 9 וַיִּזְכֹּר יוֹסֵף אֵת הַחֲלֹמוֹת
אֲשֶׁר חָלַם לָהֶם וַיֹּאמֶר אֲלֵהֶם מְרַגְּלִים אַתֶּם לִרְאוֹת אֶת־עֶרְוַת
הָאָרֶץ בָּאתֶם׃

Now Yosef was governor over the land - and it was he who held market for all the people of the land. Yosef's brothers came and bowed before him - with their faces to the ground. Yosef saw his brothers and recognized them - but he acted like stranger to them and spoke harshly to them. He said to them:

"From where have you come?"

They said: "From the land of Canaan to buy food."
Even though Yosef recognized his brothers, they did not recognize him.
And Yosef remembered the dream which he had dreamt of them.
He said to them: "You are spies! You have come to see the nakedness of the land!"

1. Read the text closely - can you figure out why Yosef hides his identity from his brothers.

___

___

___

2. Do you think this is the right thing to do?

___

___

___

ABRAVANEL ASKS:

Why did Yosef denounce his brother? It seems criminal to take vengeance or bear a grudge. Though they had intended evil - God had already turned it to good. What justification did he have for taking vengeance after 20 years. How could he ignore their plight in a strange land and that of their families suffering in famine and waiting for them?

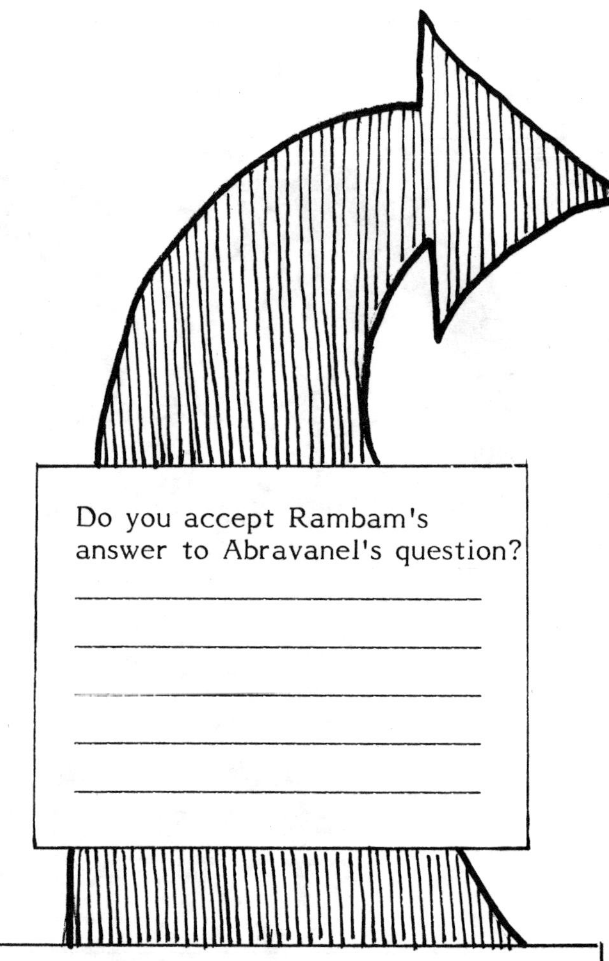

Do you accept Rambam's answer to Abravanel's question?

____

____

____

____

____

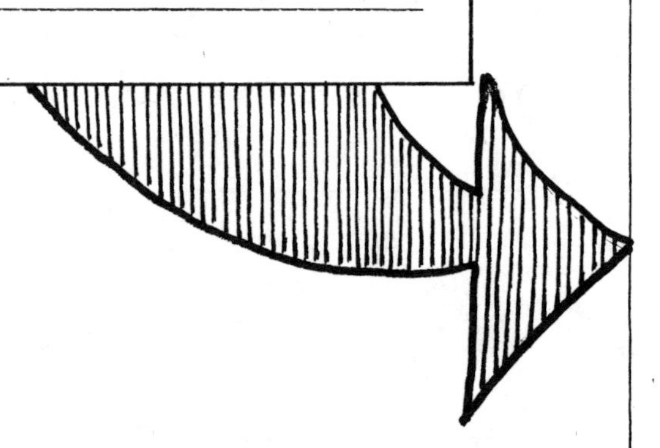

Do you have an answer to Abravanel?

____

____

____

____

____

RAMBAM ANSWERS:

This text states that when Yosef saw his brothers he remembered his dreams and noted that they had not yet been fulfilled. He understood that the first dream meant that sheaves of grain who bowed down represented all his brothers who would bow down. The second dream with the sun, moon and eleven stars meant that both his parents and his brothers would bow down to him...Yosef carried out everything in the appropriate manner in order to fulfill the dreams knowing that they would really come true.

R. ISAAC ARAMA QUESTIONS:

I am astonished at Rambam's explanation that Yosef did what he did in order to make his dreams come true. How could this benefit him? Even if it was for his benefit - he should not have sinned against his father. As for the dreams - he should have let God who sent them - make them come true. It seems infinitely foolish for a man to try to fulfill his dreams - which are matters beyond his control.

How does Yosef's deception make it possible for his brothers to demonstrate repentance?______

____

____

Do you accept Nechama Leibowitz's solution?

____

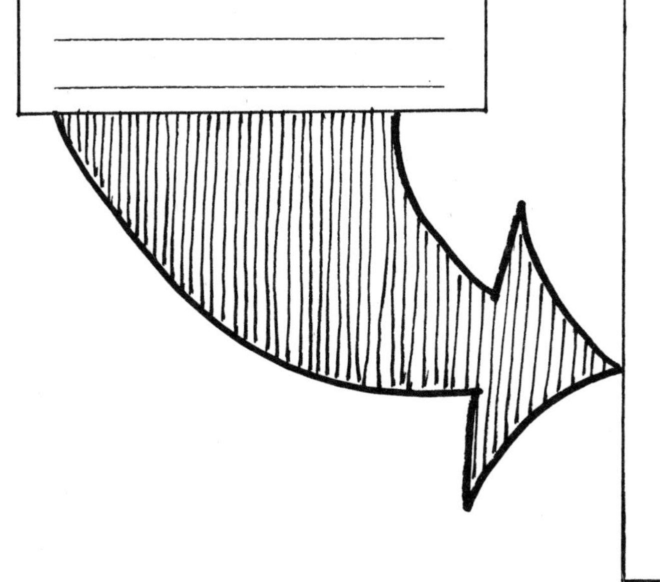

Do you agree with R. Isaac Arama's objection? Or do you think Rambam is right? Why?______________

____

____

____

____

NEḤAMA LEIBOWITZ ANSWERS:

Neḥama quotes Rambam:

What is complete repentance? It is when one is confronted by the identical thing which s/he did wrong before - and it is possible for him/her to repeat the thing but nonetheless s/he doesn't do it. If s/he refrains and does not sin, this is a true act of repentance. (Rambam)

Through his actions..."the brothers could be considered true penitents and Yosef would be able to make himself known to his brothers." (Neḥama Leibowitz)

EPISODE #11: THE REUNION

GEN. 46:1-4

וַיִּסַּע יִשְׂרָאֵל וְכָל־אֲשֶׁר־לוֹ וַיָּבֹא בְּאֵרָה שָּׁבַע וַיִּזְבַּח זְבָחִים
לֵאלֹהֵי אָבִיו יִצְחָק׃ וַיֹּאמֶר אֱלֹהִים ׀ לְיִשְׂרָאֵל בְּמַרְאֹת
הַלַּיְלָה וַיֹּאמֶר יַעֲקֹב ׀ יַעֲקֹב וַיֹּאמֶר הִנֵּנִי׃ וַיֹּאמֶר אָנֹכִי
הָאֵל אֱלֹהֵי אָבִיךָ אַל־תִּירָא מֵרְדָה מִצְרַיְמָה כִּי־לְגוֹי גָּדוֹל
אֲשִׂימְךָ שָׁם׃ אָנֹכִי אֵרֵד עִמְּךָ מִצְרַיְמָה וְאָנֹכִי אַעַלְךָ
גַם־עָלֹה וְיוֹסֵף יָשִׁית יָדוֹ עַל־עֵינֶיךָ׃

And Yisrael traveled with all that he had
and he came to Beersheva -
and he sacrificed sacrifices unto the God of his father - Yitzchak.
And God spoke to Yisrael in a night vision and said:
"Ya-akov, Ya-akov."
And he said: "Hineini."
And God said: "I am the mighty God, the God of Your Father,
fear not to go down to Egypt, for I will make a great nation of you there.
I will go down with you into Egypt, and I Myself will also bring you up again."

How many different questions does this text raise? Use each of these clues to identify your own questions and then work out your own answers.

CLUE #1: Usually in the book of Genesis, God is called the God of your father. What is God called here? (Any Questions?)

CLUE #2: When God talks to Yisrael, what does God call him? (No more shall your name be Ya-akov, rather, Yisrael shall be your name. Genesis 35:9-11) (Does this raise any questions?)

CLUE #3: Yisrael seems (according to God's speech) to be afraid to go to Egypt. Can you figure out why? (What verses have we seen in other parshiot which can be clues?) (Any questions?)

RASHI

RAMBAN

TO THE GOD OF HIS FATHER ISAAC:

The duty of honoring one's father is more important than that of honoring one's grandfather - therefore the sacrifices are associated with the name of Isaac and not with that of Abraham.

What question is Rashi answering?

___

___

___

What is Rashi's answer?

___

___

AND HE OFFERED SACRIFICES TO THE GOD OF HIS FATHER ISAAC:

The duty of honoring one's father is more important than honoring one's grandfather. Therefore the sacrifices are associated with the name of Isaac and not with that of Abraham. This is Rashi's understanding but it is not good enough. Jacob usually says: "The God before whom my fathers Abraham and Isaac did walk." (Gen. 48.15) Or God of my father Abraham and God of my father Isaac." (Gen. 32.10)

However, there is a clue in Genesis Rabbah 94.5. Jacob was about to go down to Egypt he saw that the exile was beginning for him and his children. He feared it - after all Avraham had given orders that Isaac was not supposed to leave the land of Israel (Gen. 24.6). Therefore Jacob was aware of the risks of leaving the land and prayed to the God of Isaac.

Why does Ramban disagree with Rashi?

___

What is the Ramban's answer?

___

JACOB, JACOB

The repetition of the name is a sign of affection.

What does Rashi think God is showing through repeating Jacob's name?

___

___

CONTINUED

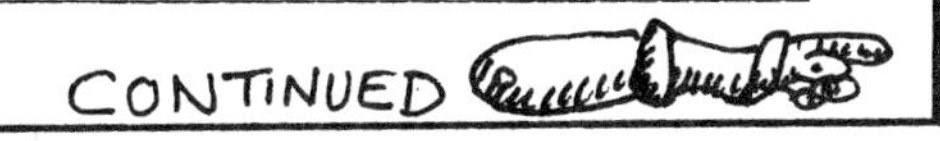

AND HE SAID: JACOB, JACOB

After God had told him, your name shall not be called Jacob anymore, but Israel shall be your name (Gen. 35.10) it would be proper that he called him by his glorious name, and so indeed it is mentioned 3 times in this section. However, once it is clear that Jacob and his family will be going into bondage, God uses the old name to signify the beginning of the period of bondage.

CONT.

Rashi (cont.)

Raban (cont.)

What does Ramban think God is showing by using the name Jacob?

FEAR NOT TO GO DOWN TO EGYPT

God said this to him because he was grieved that he was compelled to leave the land of Israel.

Why does Rashi think that Jacob is reluctant to go down to Egypt?

How can Rashi and the Ramban find such different meanings for the same passage?

Any controversy which is in the Name of Heaven is destined to create something permanent while any controversy which is not in the Name of Heaven will never result in something permenant. (Pirke Avot 5.20)

What can be gained by arguing over a Torah portion?

EPISODE 12: THE SWEARING EX. 47: 29-31

ויחי

וַיִּקְרְבוּ
יְמֵי־יִשְׂרָאֵל לָמוּת וַיִּקְרָא ׀ לִבְנוֹ לְיוֹסֵף וַיֹּאמֶר לוֹ אִם־נָא
מָצָאתִי חֵן בְּעֵינֶיךָ שִׂים־נָא יָדְךָ תַּחַת יְרֵכִי וְעָשִׂיתָ עִמָּדִי
חֶסֶד וֶאֱמֶת אַל־נָא תִקְבְּרֵנִי בְּמִצְרָיִם׃ וְשָׁכַבְתִּי עִם־אֲבֹתַי
וּנְשָׂאתַנִי מִמִּצְרַיִם וּקְבַרְתַּנִי בִּקְבֻרָתָם וַיֹּאמַר אָנֹכִי אֶעֱשֶׂה
כִדְבָרֶךָ׃ וַיֹּאמֶר הִשָּׁבְעָה לִי וַיִּשָּׁבַע לוֹ וַיִּשְׁתַּחוּ יִשְׂרָאֵל
עַל־רֹאשׁ הַמִּטָּה׃

And when the days of Yisrael's death came near
He called to his son Yosef and said to him:
"If you would please me, place your hand under my thigh as a pledge of loyalty:
Please do not bury me in Egypt,
When I lie down with my fathers, take me up from Egypt
and bury me in their burial-place."
And he said: "I will do as you have spoken."
And he said: "Swear to me."
And he swore to him. The Yisrael bowed at the head of the bed.

1. Who is "Yisrael"?

____

____

2. What burial place is he talking about?

____

____

3. Why doesn't he want to be buried in Egypt?

____

____

____

____

RASHI'S COMMENT

PLEASE DO NOT BURY ME IN EGYPT

Beneath the soil in Egypt will become filled with lice which would swarm beneath my body.

Also, those who die outside the land of Israel will not live again atthe Resurrection except after the pain caused by the body rolling through underground passages until it reaches the land of Israel.

In addition, this will prevent the Egyptians from making my tomb into a place of worship.

1. Rashi gives three explanations of why Israel does not want to be buried in Egypt. He has each ofthese spoken by Jacob to Joseph. What are these three explanations?
   a. ____________________
   b. ____________________
   c. ____________________

2. What do you think of each of these explanations?
   a. ____________________
   b. ____________________
   c. ____________________

3. Why do you think that Rashi thought that Yisrael was concerned with lice, resurrection and worship of the dead?

____

____

____

4. What messages does Rashi bring to Yisrael's request?

____

____

____

____

____

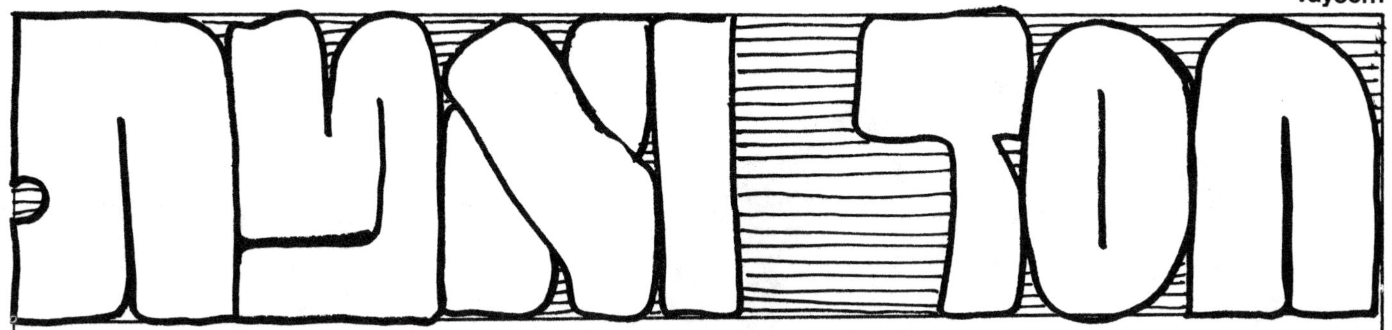

In our sidre, Ya-akov asks Yosef to do Chesed V'Emet for him. Chesed usually is translated as "Acts of lovingkindness" while "Emet" is usually translated as "truth." The words put together - Chesed shel Emet is usually used to refer to the mitzvah of caring for the dead. This is drawn from this Parasha.. Can you find the connection.

Our Rabbis taught: G'milut Chasadim is greater than tzedakah in three ways.
Acts of tzedakah involve only one's money -
G'milut chasadim can involve both money or personal service.
Tzedakah can be given only to the poor -
G'milut chasadim can be done both for the rich and the poor.
Tzedakah can be given only to the living -
G'milut chasadim can be done for both the living and the dead.

Sukkah 49b

The highest act of g'milut chasadim is that done for the dead. For with the dead there can never be any thought of being paid back. A poor person one day can be in a position to pay back a kindness, but a dead person can never repay.

Tanchuma

What kind of G'milut Chasadim can be done for the dead? Why is this a mitzvah?

____

____

____

____

____

____

____

____

EPISODE #13: THE RESISTANCE

Ex. 1: 8-22

ויקם מלך־חדש על־מצרים אשר לא־ידע את־יוסף: ויאמר
אל־עמו הנה עם בני ישראל רב ועצום ממנו: הבה נתחכמה
לו פן־ירבה והיה כי־תקראנה מלחמה ונוסף גם־הוא על־
שנאינו ונלחם־בנו ועלה מן־הארץ: וישימו עליו שרי מסים
למען ענתו בסבלתם ויבן ערי מסכנות לפרעה את־פתם
ואת־רעמסס: וכאשר יענו אתו כן ירבה וכן יפרץ ויקצו
מפני בני ישראל: ויעבדו מצרים את־בני ישראל בפרך:
וימררו את־חייהם בעבדה קשה בחמר ובלבנים ובכל־
עבדה בשדה את כל־עבדתם אשר־עבדו בהם בפרך:
ויאמר מלך מצרים למילדת העברית אשר שם האחת שפרה
ושם השנית פועה: ויאמר בילדכן את־העבריות וראיתן על־
האבנים אם־בן הוא והמתן אתו ואם־בת היא וחיה:

ותיראן
המילדת את־האלהים ולא עשו כאשר דבר אליהן מלך
מצרים ותחיין את־הילדים: ויקרא מלך־מצרים למילדת
ויאמר להן מדוע עשיתן הדבר הזה ותחיין את־הילדים:
ותאמרן המילדת אל־פרעה כי לא כנשים המצרית העברית
כי־חיות הנה בטרם תבוא אלהן המילדת וילדו: וייטב
אלהים למילדת וירב העם ויעצמו מאד: ויהי כי־יראו
המילדת את־האלהים ויעש להם בתים: ויצו פרעה לכל־
עמו לאמר כל־הבן הילוד היארה תשליכהו וכל־הבת
תחיון:

And B'nai Yisrael were fruitful
and increased abundantly
and multiplied
and waxed exceedingly mighty
and the land was filled with them.

Now there arose a new King over Egypt
He didn't know Yosef.
And He said to his people: "Hinei,
B'nai Yisrael are too many and too mighty for us.
Come let us deal wisely with them - so that
they cannot multiply - and if a war happens -
join with our enemies and fight against us.
And so, get themselves out of the land."

So,
they put taskmasters over them - to afflict them with work-burdens
and they built for Pharaoh the store cities of Pitom and Raamses.

BUT THE MORE THEY AFFLICTED THEM
THE MORE THEY MULTIPLIED
AND THE MORE THEY SPREAD OUT...

CONTINUED

And the Egyptians made B'nai Yisrael serve with rigor.

And they made their lives bitter with hard service - working with mortar and bricks and all kinds of work in the field...

And the king of Egypt spoke to the Hebrew midwives - saying to them:
"When you serve as midwives to the Hebrew women - look at the newborn,
if it is a male you shall kill him, but if it is a female - let her live.
But the midwives feared God, and did not do as the King of Egypt commanded.
They let the males live...

And Pharaoh ordered all his people - saying:
"Every son that is born you shall throw into the river
and every daughter you shall let live.

List the ways the Torah describes what happens to the population of B'nai Yisrael.	List the things that the Egyptians did in response to the population growth.
1. ______	1. ______
2. ______	2. ______
3. ______	3. ______
4. ______	4. ______
5. ______	5. ______

How many items are there in both lists?______

How does the Torah connect these two sets of events?______

______

Why do the Egyptians want to afflict B'nai Yisrael?______

______

______

And the King of Egypt spoke to the Hebrew midwives/midwives to the Hebrews saying to them:
"When you serve as midwives to the Hebrew women - look at the newborn, if it is a male you shall kill him, but if it is a female - let her live.
But the midwives feared God, and did not do as the King of Egypt commanded. They let the males live.

1. What is a midwife?

____

____

2. If the text is translated "Hebrew Midwives" - what nationality are the women?

____

3. If the text is translated "Midwives to the Hebrews" - what nationality are the women?

____

4. What might lead you to believe that the midwives were Jews?

____

____

5. What might lead you to question if they could be Jews?

____

____

6. Which translation do you think is right?

____

SOTA 11B

Rav and Shmuel:
One said: The midwives were a mother and daughter.
The other said: The midwives were a mother and a daughter-in-law.
The first thought that they were Yocheved and Miriam (Moses' mother and sister).
The other thought that they were Yocheved and Elisheva (Aaron's wife).

Which translation did Rav and Shmuel accept?

____

____

Why do you think they wanted to call the midwives Yocheved, Miriam and Elisheva even though the Torah names them Shifrah and Pu-ah?

____

____

IMREI NO'AM (A MIDRASH)

Shifrah and Puah were originally Egyptians who later came to accept Judaism.
If they were Jewish - Pharoah could have never ordered them to kill other Jews.
No one could expect them to agree to this.
This is why the Torah says: "But the midwives feared God." This teaches that at first they were heathens, but they came to accept God's law."

Which translation does this text accept?

____

Explain why it accepts this translation?

____

____

What kind of feelings do these two explanations express of non-Jews?

____

____

____

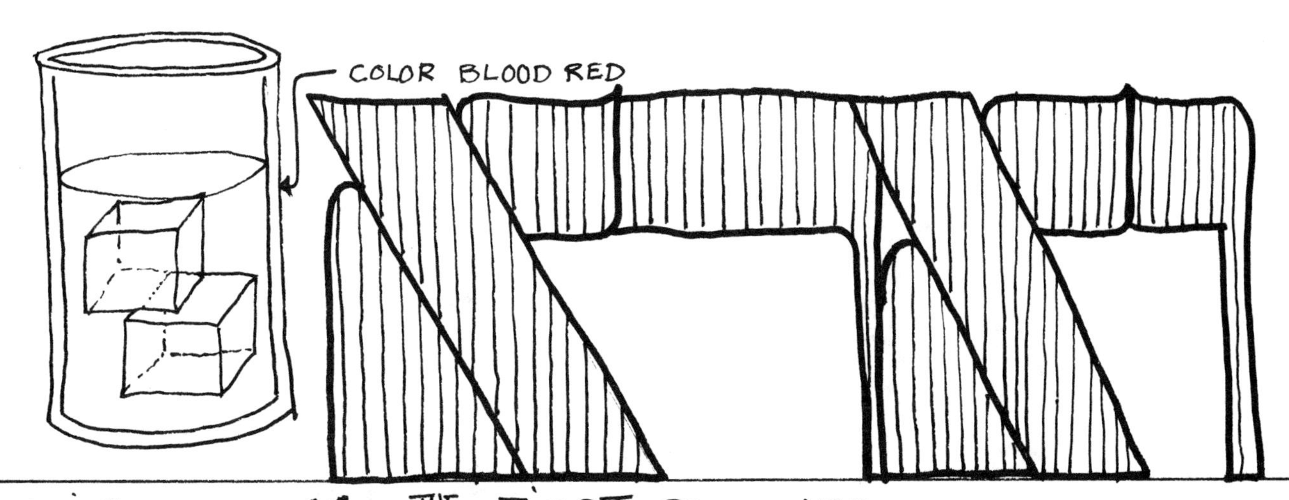

EPISODE #14: THE FIRST PLAGUES Ex. 6:6-8, 7.4-5

לָכֵן אֱמֹר לִבְנֵי־יִשְׂרָאֵל
אֲנִי יְהוָה וְהוֹצֵאתִי אֶתְכֶם מִתַּחַת סִבְלֹת מִצְרַיִם וְהִצַּלְתִּי
אֶתְכֶם מֵעֲבֹדָתָם וְגָאַלְתִּי אֶתְכֶם בִּזְרוֹעַ נְטוּיָה וּבִשְׁפָטִים
גְּדֹלִים׃ וְלָקַחְתִּי אֶתְכֶם לִי לְעָם וְהָיִיתִי לָכֶם לֵאלֹהִים
וִידַעְתֶּם כִּי אֲנִי יְהוָה אֱלֹהֵיכֶם הַמּוֹצִיא אֶתְכֶם מִתַּחַת
סִבְלוֹת מִצְרָיִם׃ וְהֵבֵאתִי אֶתְכֶם אֶל־הָאָרֶץ

(God said to Moshe)
I am the Lord:
I will bring you out from under the burden of the Egyptians
and I will deliver you from their bondage,
and I will redeem you WITH AN OUTSTRETCHED ARM,
and with great judgements
and I will take you to Me for a people
and I will be to you a God -

And you shall know that I am the Lord your God who brought
you out from under the burdens of the Egyptians
And I will bring you into the land.

1. How many things does God promise to Israel? List them:
   a. ______________________________
   b. ______________________________
   c. ______________________________
   d. ______________________________
   e. ______________________________

2. How come some scholars think there are four and others see five?

____

____

CONTINUED

3. What image (word-picture) is used for God taking Israel out of Egypt? Can you see how this image is drawn in Torah-Toons?

____

____

EX. 7:4-5

וְנָתַתִּי אֶת־יָדִי בְּמִצְרָיִם וְהוֹצֵאתִי אֶת־צִבְאֹתַי אֶת־עַמִּי
בְנֵי־יִשְׂרָאֵל מֵאֶרֶץ מִצְרַיִם בִּשְׁפָטִים גְּדֹלִים׃ וְיָדְעוּ מִצְרַיִם
כִּי־אֲנִי יְהוָה בִּנְטֹתִי אֶת־יָדִי עַל־מִצְרָיִם וְהוֹצֵאתִי אֶת־
בְּנֵי־יִשְׂרָאֵל מִתּוֹכָם׃

(And the Lord said):
I shall set my hand against Egypt - and release my troops -
My children of Israel with great judgments
And the Egyptians shall know that I am the Lord
when I stretch out My hand over Egypt
and release B'nai Yisrael from their midst.

1. What image (word picture) is used here?

____

____

2. What evidence in this text can you find, that God wanted to punish the Egyptians?

____

____

____

3. What evidence can you find in this text, that God wanted to teach the Egyptians?

____

____

____

____

MIDRASH AHEAD

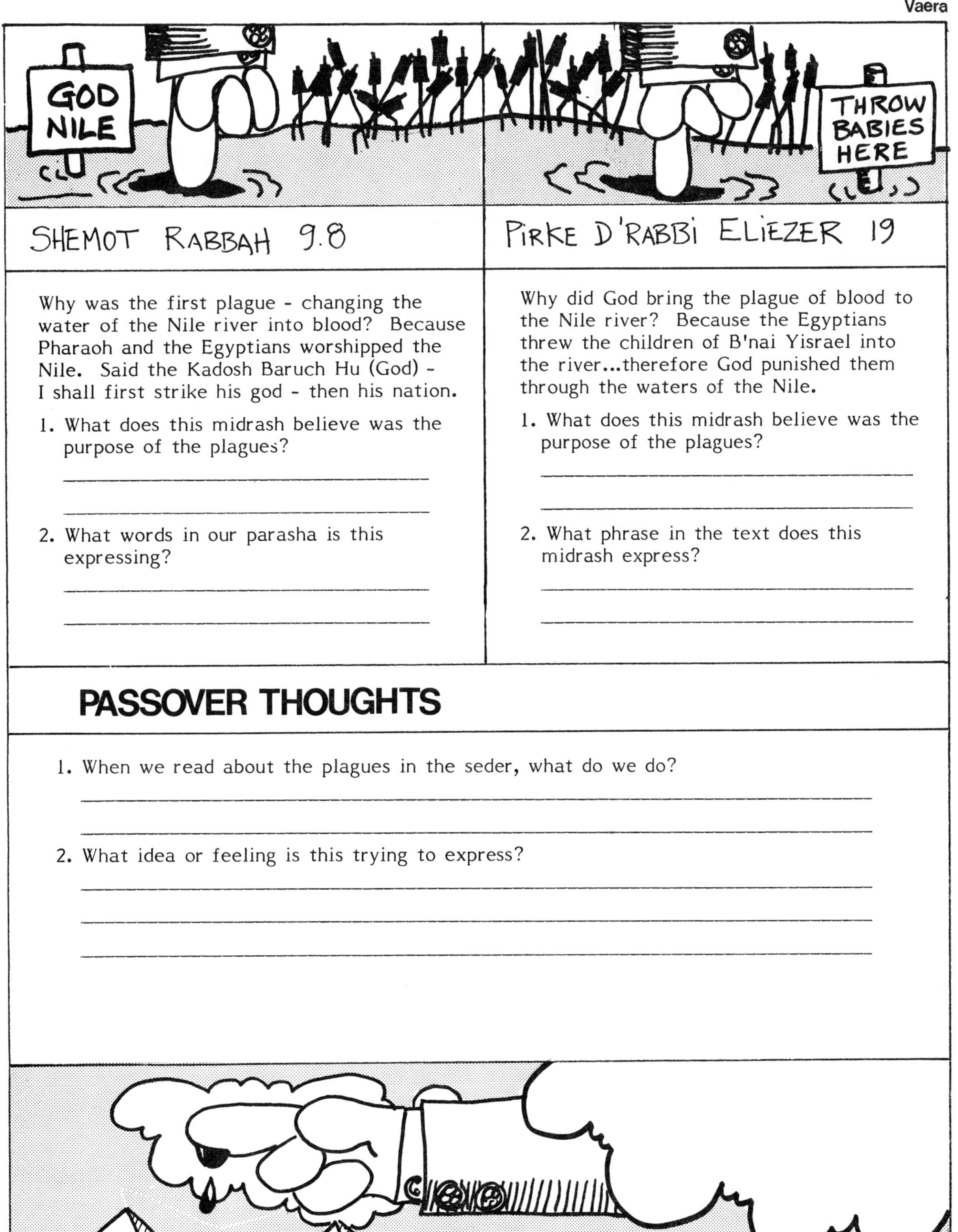

SHEMOT RABBAH 9.8

Why was the first plague - changing the water of the Nile river into blood? Because Pharaoh and the Egyptians worshipped the Nile. Said the Kadosh Baruch Hu (God) - I shall first strike his god - then his nation.

1. What does this midrash believe was the purpose of the plagues?

____

____

2. What words in our parasha is this expressing?

____

____

PIRKE D'RABBI ELIEZER 19

Why did God bring the plague of blood to the Nile river? Because the Egyptians threw the children of B'nai Yisrael into the river...therefore God punished them through the waters of the Nile.

1. What does this midrash believe was the purpose of the plagues?

____

____

2. What phrase in the text does this midrash express?

____

____

PASSOVER THOUGHTS

1. When we read about the plagues in the seder, what do we do?

____

____

2. What idea or feeling is this trying to express?

____

____

____

PUNISHMENT

Write down the story of one time you were punished when it really did you some good.

Write down the story of one time when you were punished when it really didn't do any good at all.

When is punishment good?

When isn't punishment good?

Use the "rules" you've defined and decide if the plagues were "good" punishment.

EPISODE # 15: THE EXITING

EXODUS 11:1-3

וַיֹּאמֶר יְהוָה אֶל־מֹשֶׁה עוֹד נֶגַע אֶחָד אָבִיא עַל־פַּרְעֹה
וְעַל־מִצְרַיִם אַחֲרֵי־כֵן יְשַׁלַּח אֶתְכֶם מִזֶּה כְּשַׁלְּחוֹ כָּלָה
גָּרֵשׁ יְגָרֵשׁ אֶתְכֶם מִזֶּה׃ דַּבֶּר־נָא בְּאָזְנֵי הָעָם וְיִשְׁאֲלוּ
אִישׁ ׀ מֵאֵת רֵעֵהוּ וְאִשָּׁה מֵאֵת רְעוּתָהּ כְּלֵי־כֶסֶף וּכְלֵי
זָהָב׃ וַיִּתֵּן יְהוָה אֶת־חֵן הָעָם בְּעֵינֵי מִצְרָיִם גַּם ׀ הָאִישׁ
מֹשֶׁה גָּדוֹל מְאֹד בְּאֶרֶץ מִצְרַיִם בְּעֵינֵי עַבְדֵי־פַרְעֹה וּבְעֵינֵי
הָעָם׃

And the Lord said to Moshe:
"I will bring one more plague upon Pharaoh
and upon Egypt -
afterward he will let you go -
He will definitely throw all of you out.
Speak now in the ears of the people,
and have each man ask of his neighbor
and have every woman ask of her neighbor
for gold, silver and jewels."
And the Lord gave the people
favor in the eyes of the Egyptians.

1. What does God have Moshe tell the people to do?

____

____

2. Why might this be considered theft?

____

____

3. What reasons can you come up with why this might not be theft, but a fair thing for B'nai Yisrael to do? (Use anything you know about the Exodus to help you)

____

____

____

Each of these Jewish commentaries tries to show how this command by God wasn't an order to steal from the Egyptians - but rather the expression of something fair. Explain each theory in your own words.

JOSEPHUS (Jewish Historian)

The Egyptians honored them with these gifts in order to hasten their departure (and prevent any more plagues) - others gave out of good neighborliness and friendship. When B'nai Yisrael went forth from Egypt, many Egyptians wept and felt guilty for the way they had treated B'nai Yisrael.

____

____

____

RASHBAM (Medieval commentator)

They were requested as an outright gift and not a loan. These gifts were to replace the houses, fields and moveable goods that B'nai Yisrael had to leave behind when they left Egypt.

____

____

____

____

MIDRASH CHEMDATE HA YAMIN

Why were the women instructed? Pharaoh had decreed that "every new born male be thrown in the Nile." The daughters of Israel bribed the Egyptian officials and kept their babies. The gifts they asked for their money and jewels in return.

____

____

____

CASSUTO (Modern Italian Scholar)

The Hebrew-slaves had worked for their masters for the number of years which had been predetermined by God. They were entitled to their freedom and therefore at the same time - to a farewell gratuity. Absolute justice demands it. In this case God, knowing that it would not take the place without the Israelites actions, saw to it that they asked for that which was coming to them.

____

1. Which of these explanations do you think are possible?

2. Do you think that any one of them is best?

3. Did you come up with another good idea?

4. Why do you think that all these commentators were concerned in proving that the Jews weren't stealing?

THOUGHT QUESTION

What other things do you think B'nai Yisrael should have taken from Egypt?

EPISODE #16: THE EXODUSING

EXODUS 14.5-6

וַיֻּגַּד לְמֶלֶךְ מִצְרַיִם כִּי
בָרַח הָעָם וַיֵּהָפֵךְ לְבַב פַּרְעֹה וַעֲבָדָיו אֶל־הָעָם וַיֹּאמְרוּ
מַה־זֹּאת עָשִׂינוּ כִּי־שִׁלַּחְנוּ אֶת־יִשְׂרָאֵל מֵעָבְדֵנוּ׃ וַיֶּאְסֹר
אֶת־רִכְבּוֹ וְאֶת־עַמּוֹ לָקַח עִמּוֹ׃

And it was told to the King of Egypt
that the people were fleeing -
And the heart of Pharaoh and of his servants
was turned towards the people - and they said:
"What have we done, letting B'nai Yisrael leave from serving us?"
And he made ready his chariot - and took his people with him.
And he took six-hundred of his chosen chariot-drivers, and
all the chariots of Egypt
and captains over them all.

1. Why is it that Pharaoh is angry about B'nai Yisrael leaving?

____

____

____

2. What about the wording led some people think that Pharaoh harnessed his own chariot? If he did, what would be unusual?

____

____

____

____

____

And God said: Take your son, your only son, whom you love, Isaac, and go to the land of Moriah...And Avraham arose early in the morning, and saddled his ass.

And Yosef made ready his chariot, and went up to meet Yisrael, his father, to Goshen, and he presented himself to him, and they hugged and wept a long time.

And Bilam rose up in the morning, and saddled his ass, and went with the princes of Moab.

And he made ready his chariot - and took his people with him. And he took six hundred of his chosen chariot-drivers, and all the chariots of Egypt and captains over them all.

Look at each of these four commentaries - put their explanations in your own words:

TEXT #1 - MEKHILTA (A Midrash)

Four made ready joyfully
  Avraham saddled his ass, Yosef made ready his chariot
  Bilam rose up early and saddled his ass, Pharaoh made ready his chariot
Avraham cancels out Bilam and Yosef cancels out Pharaoh.

____

____

1. What connects these four characters?

____

____

2. What does the text mean by Avraham cancels out Bilam, etc.?

____

____

3. Does this midrash believe that Pharaoh readied his own chariot?

____

__________________________________ CONTINUED

TEXT #2 - BERESHIT RABBAH (A Midrash)

Hate disrupts protocol. He had plenty of slaves, but hate disrupts protocol.

How does this midrash explain the actions of the other 3 Biblical characters (Avraham, Bilam and Yosef)?

TEXT #3 - MEKHILTA (A Midrash)

He did it with his own hand. Kings usually stand by, while others prepare their chariot and harness it. But Pharaoh, the wicked, prepared and harnessed his own chariot. As soon as his courtiers saw what he was doing, they followed suit and also made ready.

TEXT #4 - IBN EZRA (A commentator)

He made ready - in the imperative sense - meaning he caused others to make ready, just like in 1 Kings 6:14 - "Solomon built the house (Temple)" - meaning that Solomon was responsible for the Temple's construction.

THOUGHT QUESTIONS

What things do you always prepare for yourself?

EPISODE # 17: THE 9/10 COMMANDMENTS EX. 20.1FF

I am the Lord your God
You shall not make for yourself an engraved image to worship
You shall not swear falsely by the name of the Lord your God
Remember the Sabbath day to keep it holy
Honor your father and your mother
You shall not murder
You shall not commit adultery
You shall not steal
You shall not bear false witness
You shall not covet anything which belongs to your neighbor

How many commandments can you count here? ______________________

אָנֹכִי יְהוָה אֱלֹהֶיךָ אֲשֶׁר הוֹצֵאתִיךָ מֵאֶרֶץ מִצְרַיִם מִבֵּית עֲבָדִים׃

I am the Lord your God
who brought you out of the land of Egypt
out of the house of bondage.

1. Do you think that this is a commandment (mitzvah)? Why?

____

____

____

____

____

____

Restate each of these arguments in your own words:

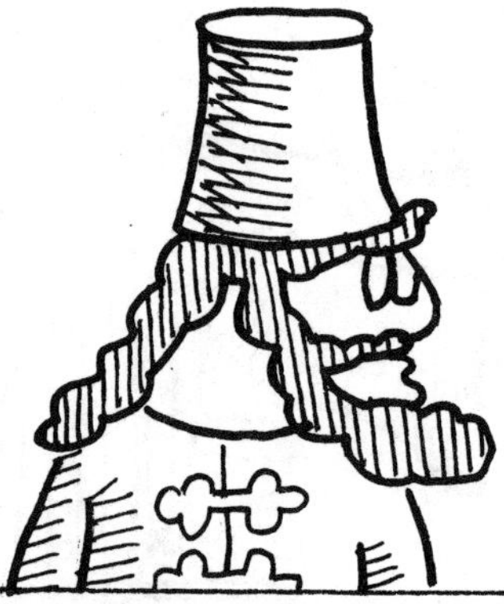

ABRAVANEL	RAMBAM
The phrase: "I am the Lord your God..." is not a commandment - either in dogma or in action. It is simply an introduction to the following commandments and rules - a statement being addressed to B'nai Yisrael letting them know who is talking to them. Ad Loc	The first mitzvah is that God commanded us to believe in God - that is we are required to believe that there is a cause and organizing force behind all existing things. This idea is expressed in the statement: "I am the Lord your God." Sefer Ha Mitzvot, 1
______________________________	______________________________
______________________________	______________________________
______________________________	______________________________
______________________________	______________________________
______________________________	______________________________

RAMBAM believed that it was a Mitzvah for Jews to believe certain things and he listed thirteen beliefs. Are there things you think a Jew should believe?

1. ______________________________
2. ______________________________
3. ______________________________
4. ______________________________
5. ______________________________
6. ______________________________
7. ______________________________
8. ______________________________
9. ______________________________
10. ______________________________
11. ______________________________
12. ______________________________
13. ______________________________

Rambam believed not only that Jews had to believe in God, but that there was a list of 13 things which Jews had to believe in. Look at this list and decide: (1) if you believe in the principle and (2) if you think all Jews should believe in it.

1. I believe that God created everything and is the only creator.

2. I believe that God is one - and the only God.

3. I believe that God has no physical form and is free from all physical properties.

4. I believe that God is the first thing and the last thing that ever was or will be.

5. I believe that God is the only One to pray to.

6. I believe that all that God told the prophets is true.

7. I believe that all that God taught Moshe was true.

8. I believe that God gave the whole Torah - just the way we have it now - to Moshe.

9. I believe that the Torah will not be changed - and that it is the perfect law.

10. I believe that God knows the actions and thoughts of all people.

11. I believe that God rewards those who perform mitzvot and punishes those who break them.

12. I believe that the messiah will come.

13. I believe that God will revive all the dead at the end of time.

EPISODE #18 THE RULES

EXODUS 21.1 FF.

21:1-3

Now these are the ordinances which you shall set before them

If you buy a Hebrew slave
he shall serve six years
and in the seventh he shall
go free without payment.

If he entered by himself
he shall go out by himself.
If he was married then
his wife shall go free with him.

וְאֵלֶּה הַמִּשְׁפָּטִים אֲשֶׁר תָּשִׂים לִפְנֵיהֶם: כִּי תִקְנֶה עֶבֶד
עִבְרִי שֵׁשׁ שָׁנִים יַעֲבֹד וּבַשְּׁבִעִת יֵצֵא לַחָפְשִׁי חִנָּם: אִם־
בְּגַפּוֹ יָבֹא בְּגַפּוֹ יֵצֵא אִם־בַּעַל אִשָּׁה הוּא וְיָצְאָה אִשְׁתּוֹ
עִמּוֹ:

22:20-22

A STRANGER you shall not harass
neither shall you oppress a STRANGER
for you were STRANGERS in the
land of Egypt.

You shall not afflict any widow or orphan.

If you hurt them in any way
if they cry at all to Me - I will
surely hear their cry.

וְגֵר לֹא־תוֹנֶה וְלֹא תִלְחָצֶנּוּ כִּי־גֵרִים הֱיִיתֶם בְּאֶרֶץ מִצְרָיִם:
כָּל־אַלְמָנָה וְיָתוֹם לֹא תְעַנּוּן: אִם־עַנֵּה תְעַנֶּה אֹתוֹ כִּי
אִם־צָעֹק יִצְעַק אֵלַי שָׁמֹעַ אֶשְׁמַע צַעֲקָתוֹ:

22:24

If you lend money to any of My people -
especially to the poor among you,
You shall not be as a creditor
neither shall you charge him interest.

אִם־כֶּסֶף ׀ תַּלְוֶה אֶת־עַמִּי אֶת־הֶעָנִי עִמָּךְ לֹא־תִהְיֶה לוֹ
כְּנֹשֶׁה לֹא־תְשִׂימוּן עָלָיו נֶשֶׁךְ:

23:6-9

You shall not favor the poor in judgment.
Keep far from a false matter and do not
bring death on the innocent righteous
for I will not acquit the wrongdoer.
Do not take bribes for bribes blind the
clear-sighted and upset the pleas of the just.

You shall not oppress a STRANGER,
for you know the feelings of the STRANGER,
for you were STRANGERS in the land of Egypt.

לֹא תַטֶּה מִשְׁפַּט אֶבְיֹנְךָ
בְּרִיבוֹ: מִדְּבַר־שֶׁקֶר תִּרְחָק וְנָקִי וְצַדִּיק אַל־תַּהֲרֹג
כִּי לֹא־אַצְדִּיק רָשָׁע: וְשֹׁחַד לֹא תִקָּח כִּי הַשֹּׁחַד יְעַוֵּר
פִּקְחִים וִיסַלֵּף דִּבְרֵי צַדִּיקִים: וְגֵר לֹא תִלְחָץ וְאַתֶּם
יְדַעְתֶּם אֶת־נֶפֶשׁ הַגֵּר כִּי־גֵרִים הֱיִיתֶם בְּאֶרֶץ מִצְרָיִם:

TEXT # 1 Ex. 22.20	A STRANGER you shall not harass neither shall you oppress a STRANGER for you were STRANGERS in the Land of Egypt.
TEXT # 2 Ex. 23.9	You shall not oppress a STRANGER, for you know the feelings of the STRANGER, for you were STRANGERS in the Land of Egypt.

In the two verses, the same basic rule about STRANGERS seems to be repeated three times. What different things do you think each of these three phrases is trying to teach?

a. A STRANGER you shall not harass ______________________

b. Neither...oppress a STRANGER ______________________

c. You shall not oppress a STRANGER ______________________

Read the comments of these two commentators:

RASHBAM

A STRANGER you shall not harass - means you shall not harass him with money matters.

Neither...oppress a STRANGER means to oppress him/her when s/he is working for you (as a slave) since they have no one to champion their cause.

BECHOR SHOR

Also you shall not oppress a STRANGER means in court.

What do these three phrases teach about?

a. Not harass = ______________________

b. Not oppress = ______________________

c. Not oppress (II) = ______________________

How do they find these answers? (Clue: Look either at Chapters 22-23 of Exodus or at worksheet #1)

____

____

____

What new skill about Torah study does this teach us?

____

____

____

Look at these biblical verses. What "connects" them?

And God said to Avram: "Know that your descendants will be STRANGERS in a land which is not theirs... Genesis 15:13	You shall not oppress you NEIGHBOR nor rob him/her. Exodus 19:13
Then Avraham rose from beside his dead... "I am a STRANGER and a settler here with you." Genesis 23:4	You shall not stand idly by the blood of your NEIGHBOR. Exodus 19:16
She bore a son who he (Moshe) named Gershom, and he said, "I have been a STRANGER in a STRANGE land." Exodus 2:22	You shall love your NEIGHBOR as yourself. Exodus 19:19
There shall be one law among you for the citizen and for the STRANGER who dwells with you. Exodus 12:49	When you come into your NEIGHBOR'S vineyard, you may eat as many grapes as you want, but you shall not put any in a container... Deuteronomy 23:25
You shall not harass a STRANGER... Exodus 20:20	When you lend your NEIGHBOR any kind of loan, you shall not go into his/her house to receive his/her pledge. Rather you should wait outside for the pledge to be brought to you. Deuteronomy 24:10

1. Who are your neighbors?

____

____

2. What people are strangers to you?

____

____

3. What do you think the Torah wants you to do with strangers and neighbors?

____

____

____

____

EPISODE # 19: THE MISHKAN EX. 25.1-9

And the Lord spoke to Moses - saying:
"Speak to the children of Israel - That they take an offering for Me
from every person whose heart is willing.
And this is the offering which you shall take:
Gold and silver and brass,
blue, purple and scarlet
fine linen, goats' hair, rams' skins dyed red
sealskins
and acacia wood
oil for light, spices for the anointing oil and for the sweet incense,
onyx stones and stones to be set for the ephod and for the breast plate.

Let them make ME a sanctuary - and I will dwell within THEM.

וַיְדַבֵּר יְהוָה אֶל־מֹשֶׁה לֵּאמֹר׃ דַּבֵּר אֶל־בְּנֵי יִשְׂרָאֵל
וְיִקְחוּ־לִי תְּרוּמָה מֵאֵת כָּל־אִישׁ אֲשֶׁר יִדְּבֶנּוּ לִבּוֹ תִּקְחוּ
אֶת־תְּרוּמָתִי׃ וְזֹאת הַתְּרוּמָה אֲשֶׁר תִּקְחוּ מֵאִתָּם זָהָב
וָכֶסֶף וּנְחֹשֶׁת׃ וּתְכֵלֶת וְאַרְגָּמָן וְתוֹלַעַת שָׁנִי וְשֵׁשׁ וְעִזִּים׃
וְעֹרֹת אֵילִם מְאָדָּמִים וְעֹרֹת תְּחָשִׁים וַעֲצֵי שִׁטִּים׃ שֶׁמֶן
לַמָּאֹר בְּשָׂמִים לְשֶׁמֶן הַמִּשְׁחָה וְלִקְטֹרֶת הַסַּמִּים׃ אַבְנֵי־
שֹׁהַם וְאַבְנֵי מִלֻּאִים לָאֵפֹד וְלַחֹשֶׁן׃ וְעָשׂוּ לִי מִקְדָּשׁ
וְשָׁכַנְתִּי בְּתוֹכָם׃ כְּכֹל אֲשֶׁר אֲנִי מַרְאֶה אוֹתְךָ אֵת תַּבְנִית
הַמִּשְׁכָּן וְאֵת תַּבְנִית כָּל־כֵּלָיו וְכֵן תַּעֲשׂוּ׃

1. Go through this list of items and see what "professions" it would take to work with them?

____

____

____

____

2. What does this list teach you about "desert life?"

____

____

____

3. If God is everywhere - why do you think God wanted the Jewish people to build one place from which to worship God?

____

____

____

____

Look at these comments on this text. For each write down (1) how they solve the problem in the next, and (2) what message/moral/lesson they teach.

Let them make Me a sanctuary - and I will dwell within THEM.

What is the problem/question in this verse?______________________________

____

ABRAVANEL: Why does God command us to make a space for God to well in when God takes up no space? To show that God is connected to the earth and to the people.

Solution:____

Moral:____

MIDRASH TZEDAKA LA DEREKH:

The divine presence does not rest in the sanctuary on account of the sanctuary - but rather on account of Israel - for they constitute the Temple of God.

Solution:__________________________________

Moral:____________________________________

MIDRASH TANCHUMA:

The Kadosh Baruch Hu said : "Let them make me a sanctuary so that all the nations of the world will know that the deed of the Golden calf has been forgiven." Said the Kadosh Baruch Hu: "Let the gold of the Mishkan atone for the gold of the calf.

Solution:_____________________________

Moral:________________________________

ABRAVANEL: (Another comment)

In the beginning God only commanded Israel with civil laws - but after they made the Golden calf, God provided an antidote for the spiritual weakness and gave them religious laws.

Solution: ____________________

Moral: ____________________

JOEL GRISHAVER

Ira Lester Grishaver taught: The work of building the Tabernacle caused God to dwell among the people. That is why the text reads: You will MAKE me a Dwelling-place, and I will dwell within YOU. Otherwise, you would have expected God to dwell in the dwelling place.

Solution: ____________________

Moral: ____________________

THOUGHT QUESTION

List as many things as you can which synagogues do?

____

____

____

____

____

____

____

____

____

____

____

____

____

____

____

1. Which of these things "create a dwelling place for God?"

2. Which of these things turn "Israel into the Temple of God?"

3. Which of these things connect "heaven and earth?"

4. Which of these things cause "God to dwell within us?"

5. What else do these things do?

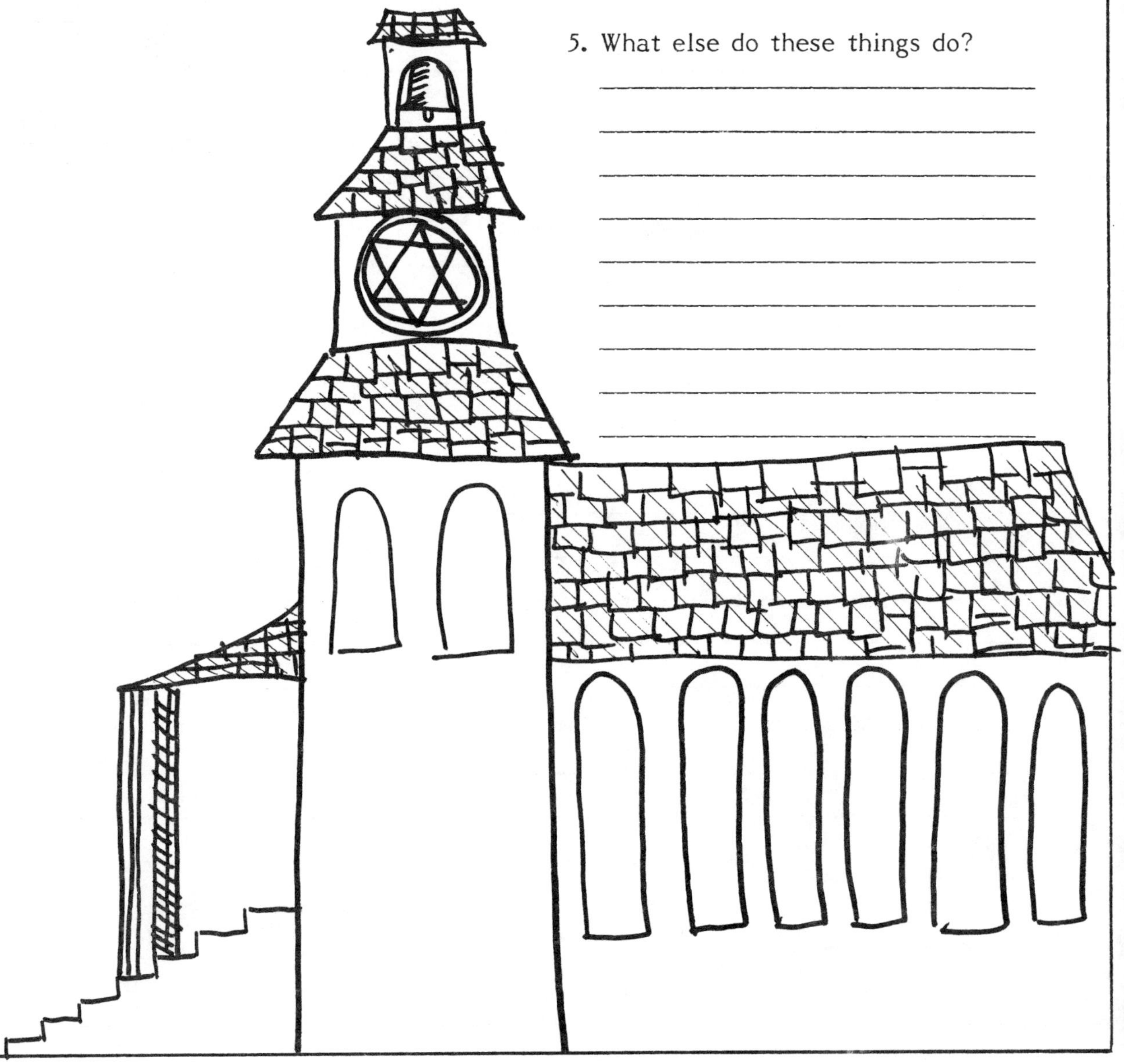

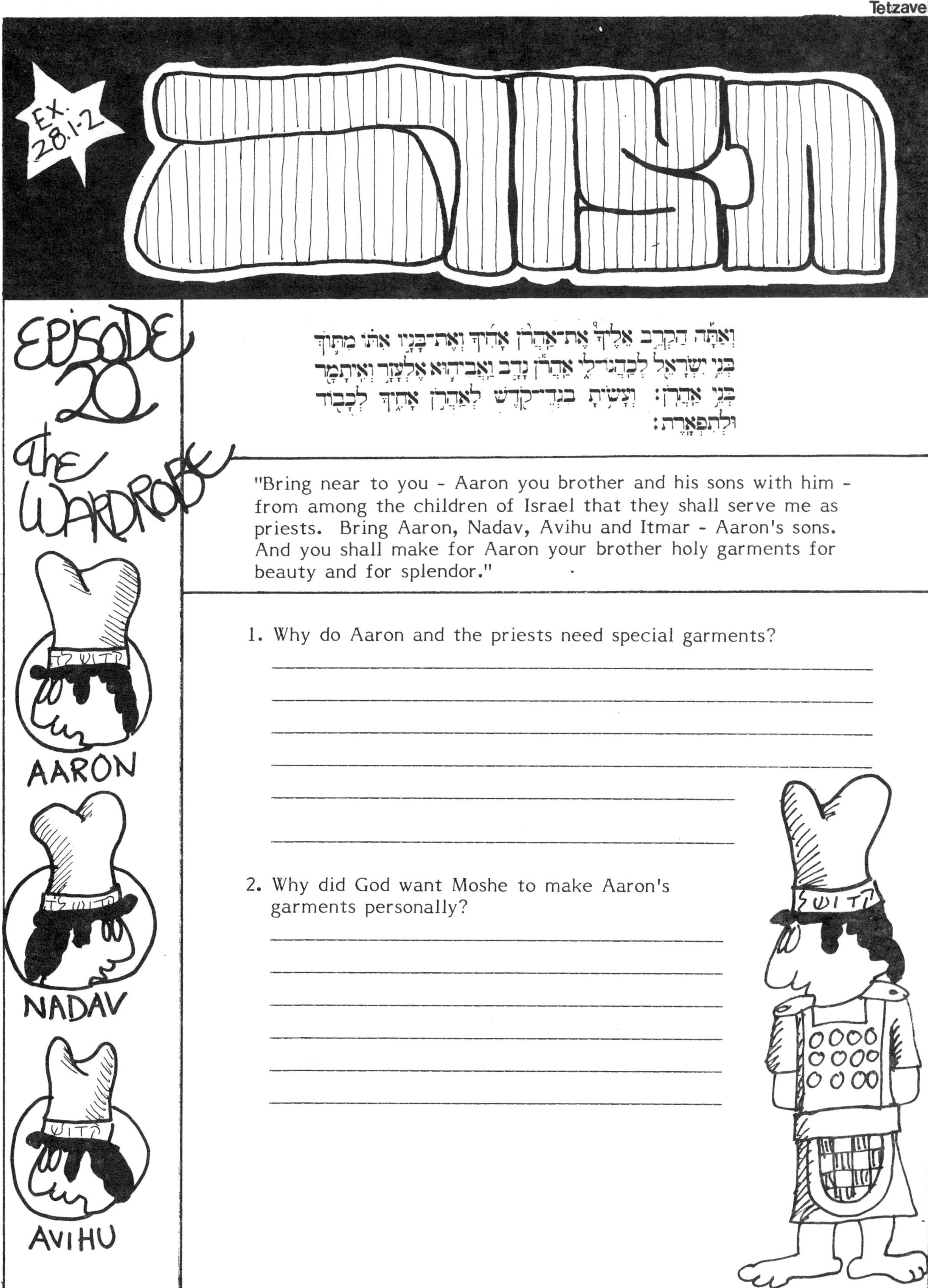

וְאַתָּה הַקְרֵב אֵלֶיךָ אֶת־אַהֲרֹן אָחִיךָ וְאֶת־בָּנָיו אִתּוֹ מִתּוֹךְ
בְּנֵי יִשְׂרָאֵל לְכַהֲנוֹ־לִי אַהֲרֹן נָדָב וַאֲבִיהוּא אֶלְעָזָר וְאִיתָמָר
בְּנֵי אַהֲרֹן׃ וְעָשִׂיתָ בִגְדֵי־קֹדֶשׁ לְאַהֲרֹן אָחִיךָ לְכָבוֹד
וּלְתִפְאָרֶת׃

"Bring near to you - Aaron you brother and his sons with him - from among the children of Israel that they shall serve me as priests. Bring Aaron, Nadav, Avihu and Itmar - Aaron's sons. And you shall make for Aaron your brother holy garments for beauty and for splendor."

1. Why do Aaron and the priests need special garments?

____

____

____

____

____

____

2. Why did God want Moshe to make Aaron's garments personally?

____

____

____

____

____

____

List two questions this text urges you to ask:

1. Why ______________________ needs special ______________________.

2. Why ______________________ Moshe himself ______________________.

Look at these comments. For each, write down (1) what question they answer, (2) how they solve the problem, and (3) what moral they teach.

MIDRASHAI HA TORAH

Moshe our teacher in humility wanted to build up the honor and glory of Aaron. He did the task himself, not like one who was commanded, but rather as one who volunteers - just like a friend doing a favor for a friend.

Question: ______________________

____

Solution: ______________________

____

Moral: ______________________

____

BENNO JACOB (20TH CENTURY)

Clothing is not merely a protection against the cold, or just decoration. It makes people different than animals. The fact that God gave clothes to Adam and Eve and dressed them shows that clothing is not just a social convention but rather an act of creation (Moshe gave clothing and dressed Aaron).

Question: ______________________

____

Solution: ______________________

____

Moral: ______________________

____

RASHI	RAMBAM

Install him in the priesthood by means of garments mentioned here - so that he can become My priest. Question:________ ________ Solution:________ ________ Moral:________ ________	This means that Aaron was to be distinguished and glorified with garments of distinction and beauty...for these garments were the same as those which a King wore in that time. Question:________ ________ Solution:________ ________ Moral:________ ________

THOUGHT QUESTION

List your five favorite pieces of clothing. What does each one make you into?

____

____

____

____

____

____

THE WELL-DRESSED TORAH

TORAH IS THE HEBREW NAME FOR THE FIRST FIVE BOOKS OF THE BIBLE.

JEWS USUALLY STUDY THE TORAH FROM EDITIONS WHICH ARE PRINTED AND BOUND LIKE REGULAR BOOKS, BUT IN EVERY SYNAGOGUE A HAND-WRITTEN **SEFER TORAH** IS KEPT IN THE ARK. THE **SEFER TORAH** IS WRITTEN ON A SCROLL AND IT IS CLOTHED IN SPECIAL GARMENTS AND ORNAMENTS AND TREATED WITH SPECIAL CEREMONY.

THE **SEFER TORAH** IS MORE THAN JUST A COPY OF THE TORAH, IT IS ALSO A SYMBOL. WE CAN LEARN A LITTLE OF WHAT THE TORAH MEANS TO US BY THE WAY THE TORAH IS DRESSED.

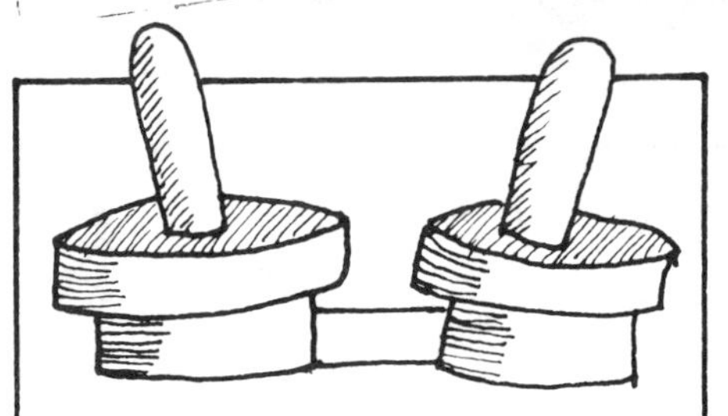

THE TORAH SCROLL IS ROLLED ON WOODEN ROLLERS CALLED AN **ETZ CHAYIM**—TREE OF LIFE.

ACCORDING TO TRADITION, TORAH IS A LIVING AND GROWING ENTITY WHICH GIVES WISDOM AND LIFE, JUST LIKE THE TREE IN THE GARDEN OF EDEN.

SOME TORAH SCROLLS COVER THE **ETZ CHAYIM** WITH FANCY ORNAMENTS. THESE ARE CALLED **RIMONIM** WHICH MEANS POMEGRANATES. SYMBOLICALLY THEY ARE THE FRUIT OF THE TREE OF LIFE.

POMEGRANATES ARE THOUGHT TO BE SPECIAL BECAUSE A FOLK TRADITION TEACHES THAT THEY HAVE 613 SEEDS. 613 IS THE NUMBER OF **MITZVOT** FOUND IN THE TORAH. THIS MAKES COMMANDMENTS THE FRUIT OF OUR STUDY.

TORAH SCROLLS ARE TIED TOGETHER WITH FANCY GIRDLES WHICH ARE CALLED TORAH BINDERS.

GERMAN JEWISH MOTHERS USED TO TAKE THEIR SONS' SWADDLING CLOTHES AND MAKE THEM INTO FANCY TORAH BINDERS CALLED WIMPLES. ON THE WIMPLE, THEY WOULD EMBROIDER OR PAINT THEIR SON'S NAME PLUS THE FOLLOWING:

"EVEN AS HE HAS BEEN ENTERED INTO THE COVENANT, SO MAY HE BE ENTERED INTO TORAH, MARRIAGE, AND A LIFE OF GOOD DEEDS."

THE WIMPLE TIED TORAH TO A JEW'S WHOLE LIFE.

OVER THE TORAH, ASHKENAZIC JEWS PLACED A FANCY OUTER COVER OF BEAUTIFUL CLOTH.

THE COVER, CALLED A MANTLE, WAS VERY MUCH A REGAL ROBE, MADE OF THE MOST EXPENSIVE CLOTH, DECORATED WITH JEWISH SYMBOLS AND SUCH ANIMALS AS LIONS AND DEER. GOLD AND SILVER THREAD AND FANCY BEADWORK WERE USED TO MAKE THE MANTLE BEAUTIFUL AND UNIQUE.

OTHER TORAH SCROLLS HAVE CROWNS PLACED ON THEIR **ETZ CHAYIM**. THIS MAKES THEM LOOK LIKE ROYALTY.

JEWISH TRADITION SPEAKS OF THE "CROWN OF TORAH," MEANING THAT A PERSON GAINS WISDOM AND SENSITIVITY FROM STUDYING TORAH.

WHEN ITALIAN JEWS MADE CROWNS FOR THE TORAH, THEY USED BOTH IDEAS: THEY MADE THE TORAH LOOK LIKE ROYALTY BY GIVING IT A CROWN AND THEY MADE THE **MITZVOT** THE FRUIT OF TORAH STUDY BY ALSO INCLUDING **RIMONIM**.

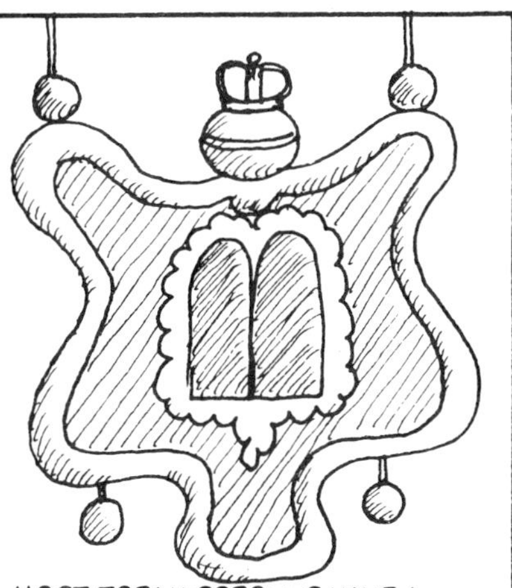

MOST TORAH SCROLLS HAVE A BREASTPLATE PLACED OVER THE MANTLE. THE BREASTPLATE WAS BOTH A BADGE OF AUTHORITY AND A SHIELD OF PROTECTION FOR THE TORAH.

SEPHARDIC JEWS PLACE GREAT EMPHASIS ON PROTECTING THEIR TORAH SCROLLS.

THEY PUT EACH TORAH IN ITS OWN CASE—JUST THE WAY THE CHILDREN OF ISRAEL PUT THE ORIGINAL TORAH IN THE ARK WHEN THEY CARRIED IT THROUGH THE WILDERNESS.

JEWS ARE CONCERNED WITH PROTECTING BOTH THE SCROLL AND THE MEANING OF THE TORAH.

THE TORAH CLEARLY DESCRIBES THE CLOTHING WORN BY THE HIGH PRIEST. (EXOD. 28)

ON HIS HEAD, THE HIGH PRIEST WORE A GOLD HEADBAND WHICH SAID: "HOLY TO THE LORD."

HIS CLOTHING BEGAN WITH AN UNDERGARMENT FOR MODESTY. THIS WAS COVERED WITH A WHITE TUNIC AND TIED WITH A GIRDLE. NEXT CAME A BLUE ROBE WITH POMEGRANATE BELLS AT THE BOTTOM.

OVER THESE WENT AN EMBROIDERED APRON (OR COVER) CALLED THE **EPHOD**. OVER THIS THE HIGH PRIEST WORE A GOLD BREASTPLATE WITH TWELVE PRECIOUS STONES, ONE FOR EACH OF THE TWELVE TRIBES.

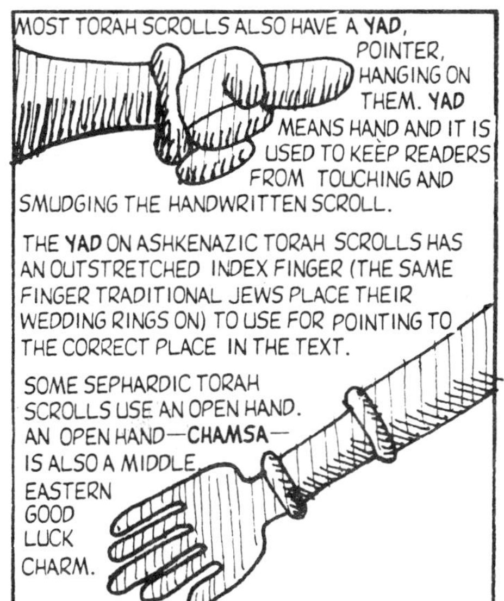
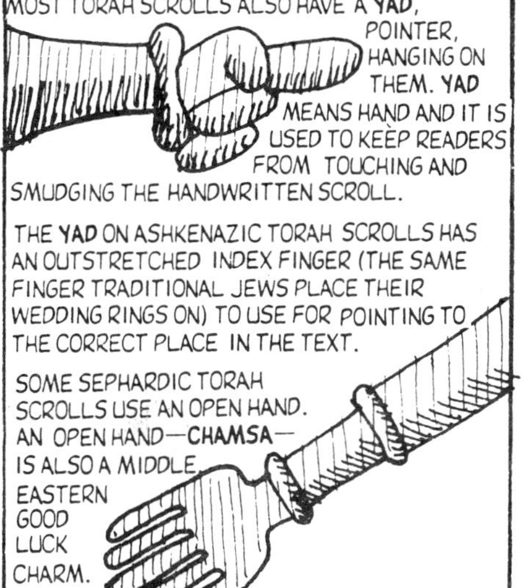

MOST TORAH SCROLLS ALSO HAVE A **YAD**, POINTER, HANGING ON THEM. **YAD** MEANS HAND AND IT IS USED TO KEEP READERS FROM TOUCHING AND SMUDGING THE HANDWRITTEN SCROLL.

THE **YAD** ON ASHKENAZIC TORAH SCROLLS HAS AN OUTSTRETCHED INDEX FINGER (THE SAME FINGER TRADITIONAL JEWS PLACE THEIR WEDDING RINGS ON) TO USE FOR POINTING TO THE CORRECT PLACE IN THE TEXT.

SOME SEPHARDIC TORAH SCROLLS USE AN OPEN HAND. AN OPEN HAND—**CHAMSA**—IS ALSO A MIDDLE EASTERN GOOD LUCK CHARM.

EPISODE #21 THE SHATTERING

EXODUS 32.19

וַיְהִי
כַּאֲשֶׁר קָרַב אֶל־הַמַּחֲנֶה וַיַּרְא אֶת־הָעֵגֶל וּמְחֹלֹת וַיִּחַר־
אַף מֹשֶׁה וַיַּשְׁלֵךְ מִיָּדָו אֶת־הַלֻּחֹת וַיְשַׁבֵּר אֹתָם תַּחַת
הָהָר׃

And it came to pass
as soon as he came near to the camp
that he saw the calf and the dancing
and Moshe's anger burned
and he hurled the tablets from his hands
and shattered them at the foot of the mountain.

1. Why did Moshe destroy the tablets?

____

____

____

____

2. How could Moshe destroy anything as Holy as the Tablets?

____

____

____

____

BAL TASHCHIT

3. If the Talmud teaches: "It is forbidden for a Jew to destroy anything which could be useful to people" - how come neither the Torah nor the Jewish tradition complains about his destroying the tablets?

____

____

____

What "problem" do the rabbis find with Moshe's behavior?

____

____

____

Why are they surprised when the Torah doesn't complain about Moshe's behavior?

____

____

____

Take a look at each of these commentaries. Fo each one explain (1) How they explain why the Torah accepts Moshe's smashing the tablets, and (2) what lesson/moral they teach from their explanations.

D'VARIM RABBAH

Moshe descended from heaven holding the Tablets. When he saw with his own eyes what was happening, "Moshe's anger burned." Said the Kadosh Baruch Hu - "Didn't you believe me that they had made a golden calf?"

Explanation: ______________________________

____

____

Moral: ______________________________

____

____

SHEMOT RABBAH

Moshe smashed the tablets in order to protect Israel. To what can this be compared - to a king who sent a servant to find him a bride. The servant did so but before the wedding contract could be signed the woman involved herself with another. What did the servant do? He tore up the contract. Better the woman be judged as an unmarried woman who did wrong than as a wife who committed adultery (Adultery was a capital crime).

Explanation: ______________________________

____

Moral: ______________________________

____

RAMBAM

Moses did not hesitate to break them because his anger was roused at the sight of their evil conduct. He could not control himself.

Explanation:________________________________

____

____

Moral:________________________________

____

____

When Moshe saw the calf - all his strength vanished. He just managed to push the tablets far enough away so that they didn't land on his feet.

Explanation:________________________________

____

____

Moral:________________________________

____

____

ISAAC ARAMA

Moshe - with deep psychological insight - didn't break the tablets on the mountain out of anger. Rather he did it at last foot of the foot of the mountain where it would make the greatest impact on B'nai Yisrael and shock them into doing t'shuva when a great treasure was lost before their eyes.

Explanation:________________________________

____

Moral:________________________________

____

BAL TASHCHIT
In this Torah portion we talked about the legal principle of BAL TASHCHIT. Let's look at how this law evolved, and how it is applied.
In the Torah it says:
When you besiege a city for a long time, making war against it in order to capture it, you shall not destroy trees (lo tashchit) by wielding the axe.
Deuteronomy 20.19
When the Rabbis work with this law, they make it more general. This is the way it is found in the TALMUD - Kiddushin 32a.
Whoever breaks vessels or tears garments or destroys a building or clogs up a well or does away with food in a destructive manner violates the mitzvah of bal tashchit (Deut. 20.19)
LIST 5 PLACES WHERE THIS RULE SHOULD BE APPLIED TODAY.
1. ____
2. ____
3. ____
4. ____
5. ____
COMMENT: ____
By the middle ages this same concept had been made into an even more general rule which can be found in the SHULCHAN ARUCH - a famous law code.
It is forbidden to destroy anything which can be useful to people.

EPISODE #22: THE GATHERING

EX. 35.25FF.

וַיַּקְהֵל מֹשֶׁה אֶת־כָּל־עֲדַת בְּנֵי יִשְׂרָאֵל וַיֹּאמֶר אֲלֵהֶם
אֵלֶּה הַדְּבָרִים אֲשֶׁר־צִוָּה יְהוָה לַעֲשֹׂת אֹתָם׃ שֵׁשֶׁת יָמִים
תֵּעָשֶׂה מְלָאכָה וּבַיּוֹם הַשְּׁבִיעִי יִהְיֶה לָכֶם קֹדֶשׁ שַׁבַּת
שַׁבָּתוֹן לַיהוָה כָּל־הָעֹשֶׂה בוֹ מְלָאכָה יוּמָת׃ לֹא־תְבַעֲרוּ
אֵשׁ בְּכֹל מֹשְׁבֹתֵיכֶם בְּיוֹם הַשַּׁבָּת׃ לוי פ
וַיֹּאמֶר מֹשֶׁה אֶל־כָּל־עֲדַת בְּנֵי־יִשְׂרָאֵל לֵאמֹר זֶה הַדָּבָר
אֲשֶׁר־צִוָּה יְהוָה לֵאמֹר׃ קְחוּ מֵאִתְּכֶם תְּרוּמָה לַיהוָה כֹּל
נְדִיב לִבּוֹ יְבִיאֶהָ אֵת תְּרוּמַת יְהוָה זָהָב וָכֶסֶף וּנְחֹשֶׁת׃

Moshe assembled all the congregation of the children of Israel - and said to them:

"These are the words which the Lord commanded you to do. Six days shall work be done, but the seventh day shall be a holy day - a shabbat of solemn rest."

And Moses spoke to all the children of Israel saying:

"Take an offering from among you to the Lord. Let all who are of a willing heart bring the Lord's offering."

1. What two rules does Moshe introduce here?

   a. ______________________________

   b. ______________________________

2. What in the words Moshe chooses might lead you to believe that these two rules are to be compared?

   ____

   ____

3. Why do you think the Torah is bringing these two rules (observing Shabbat and building the Tabernacle) together?

   ____

   ____

   ____

   ____

We know that the rabbis connected the two ideas in this passage: Observing the Shabbat and building the Mishkan. Lets see if we can follow the way they make the connection.

Then Moshe gathered all the congregation of B'nai Yisrael together and said to them:

These are the things which the Lord commanded you to do.
Six days shall work be done, but on the seventh day there shall be to you a holy day -
A Shabbat of rest - whosoever does work shall be put to death.
You shall light no fires throughout your homes on Shabbat.

Exodus 35:1-3

Why does the Torah add these laws about Shabbat before describing the donations needed to build the Mishkan?

Because the last time the list is given in Exodus 25:8 it says: "Let them make a sanctuary for Me..." I might imagine that it would be okay to build the sanctuary either on Shabbat or on weekdays.

Therefore, I should make the connection: "Let them Make me a sanctuary" on all other days but the Shabbat.

MEKHILTA

1. According to the Mekhilta, why does Moshe repeat both rules about building the Mishkan and rules about working on Shabbat?

____

____

____

____

2. The rabbis later find that 39 kinds of work were used in building the Mishkan. They make these 39 kinds of work into those which are forbidden on Shabbat. How do they make this connection?

____

____

____

____

MISHNEH SHABBAT 7:2

Look at this passage and see if you can figure out what is being discussed:

THE MAIN CLASSES OF WORK ARE 40 LESS 1:

1. Sowing
2. Ploughing
3. Reaping
4. Binding Sheaves
5. Threshing
6. Winnowing
7. Sorting
8. Grinding
9. Sifting
10. Kneading
11. Baking

12. Shearing Wool
13. Beating It
14. Bleaching It
15. Dyeing It
16. Spinning
17. Stretching the Warp
18. Making 2 Loops
19. Weaving 2 Loops
20. Separating 2 Threads
21. Tying a Knot
22. Sewing 2 Stiches
23. Tearing in order to Sew 2 Stiches
24. Untying a knot

25. Trapping a deer
26. Slaughtering It
27. Flaying It
28. Salting It
29. Curing The Hide
30. Scraping It
31. Cutting It Up

32. Writing 2 Letters
33. Erasing in order to Write 2 Letters

34. Building
35. Tearing Down
36. Putting Out a Fire
37. Lighting a Fire
38. Striking with a Hammer
39. Carrying from Domain to Domain

A. How is this list divided into sections?

____

____

____

____

____

B. What do you think this list represents?

____

____

____

____

____

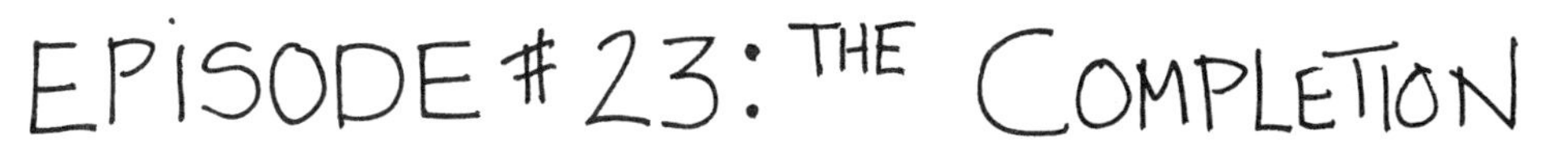

Ex. 39.21

When we look at the description of the completion of the Tabernacle, we see a number of strange things.

וַתֵּ֕כֶל
כָּל־עֲבֹדַ֕ת מִשְׁכַּ֖ן אֹ֣הֶל מוֹעֵ֑ד וַֽיַּעֲשׂוּ֙ בְּנֵ֣י יִשְׂרָאֵ֔ל כְּכֹ֡ל
אֲשֶׁ֨ר צִוָּ֧ה יְהוָ֛ה אֶת־מֹשֶׁ֖ה כֵּ֥ן עָשֽׂוּ׃

All the work of the Tabernacle of the tent of meeting was finished
and B'nai Yisrael did according to all that the Lord commanded Moshe.
So they did.

FACT: The work on the Tabernacle was done by Betzalel and a group of skilled craftsmen.

The Lord spoke to Moshe saying: "See, I have singled out by name Betzalel, son of Uri son of Hur, of the tribe of Judah. I have endowed him with a divine spirit of skill, ability, and knowledge in every kind of craft... (Ex. 31.1)

IN THE LIGHT OF THIS FACT, WHAT SEEMS STRANGE ABOUT THIS PASSAGE?

____

____

____

וַיְהִ֞י בַּחֹ֧דֶשׁ הָרִאשׁ֛וֹן בַּשָּׁנָ֥ה הַשֵּׁנִ֖ית
בְּאֶחָ֣ד לַחֹ֑דֶשׁ הוּקַ֖ם הַמִּשְׁכָּֽן׃ וַיָּ֨קֶם מֹשֶׁ֜ה אֶת־הַמִּשְׁכָּ֗ן
וַיִּתֵּן֙ אֶת־אֲדָנָ֔יו וַיָּ֙שֶׂם֙ אֶת־קְרָשָׁ֔יו וַיִּתֵּ֖ן אֶת־בְּרִיחָ֑יו וַיָּ֖קֶם
אֶת־עַמּוּדָֽיו׃

In the first month of the second year, on the first of the month
the Tabernacle was set up.
Moshe set up the Tabernacle
placing its sockets, setting up its planks, inserting its bars and errecting its posts.

FACT: EACH OF THE BOARDS FOR THE TABERNACLE WAS MORE THAN 20 FEET LONG. GIVEN THIS TEXT, WHAT IMPRESSION ARE YOU GIVEN ABOUT WHO SET IT UP.

____

When we compare these two passages we reach two interesting conclusions:
1. That all of B'nai Yisrael were given credit for building the Mishkan when only a few skilled craftsmen did the actual work.
2. That Moshe seems to be credited with setting up the Mishkan when it would have logically taken a team of people.

Here is the way Rashi comments on this passage (1) weaving these two facts together and (2) drawing from the midrash.

RASHI'S COMMENTS

AND B'NAI YISRAEL MADE
all the work of the Mishkan.
ACCORDING TO ALL THAT THE LORD
COMMANDED MOSHE.

AND THEY BROUGHT THE MISHKAN TO MOSHE
for they were unable to set it up themselves.
Because Moshe had done no work in constructing the Mishkan, the Kadosh Baruch Hu left the setting up to him, for no one was able to set it up because of the weight of the boards which no human strength was capable of lifting up. Moshe however, succeeded in placing it in position.

Moshe said to the Kadosh Baruch Hu: How can people set this up?
God answered him: You get to work.

Moshe appeared to be setting it up, but in fact the Tabernacle set itself up.
This is the Midrash of Rabbi Tanchuma.

IN QUOTING THIS MIDRASH, WHO DOES RASHI SAY IS RESPONSIBLE FOR SETTING UP THE MISKAN?

____

____

WHAT MESSAGE CAN BE LEARNED IF EACH OF THESE WAS RESPONSIBLE FOR CREATING THE TABERNACLE:

1. ALL OF ISRAEL ____________________
2. MOSHE ____________________
3. GOD ____________________

Compare these two texts. What do they have in common?

וַיְכֻלּוּ הַשָּׁמַיִם וְהָאָרֶץ	THUS WERE COMPLETED the heavens and earth	THUS WERE COMPLETED all the work of the Mishkan	וַתֵּכֶל כָּל־עֲבֹדַת מִשְׁכַּן אֹהֶל מוֹעֵד.
וְכָל־צְבָאָם	and all their host	and B'nai Yisrael did according to all the Lord commanded	וַיַּעֲשׂוּ בְּנֵי יִשְׂרָאֵל כְּכֹל אֲשֶׁר צִוָּה יְיָ ---
וַיְכַל אֱלֹהִים בַּיּוֹם הַשְּׁבִיעִי מְלַאכְתּוֹ אֲשֶׁר עָשָׂה ---	AND GOD COMPLETED on the seventh day His WORK which He had done.	AND MOSES COMPLETED the WORK.	--- וַיְכַל מֹשֶׁה אֶת־הַמְּלָאכָה.

CREATION

MISHKAN

WHAT DO YOU THINK THE TORAH IS TRYING TO TEACH BY DESCRIBING THE COMPLETION OF THE CREATION OF THE WORLD AND THE COMPLETION OF THE CREATION OF THE MISHKAN IN SIMILAR LANGUAGE?

EPISODE # 24: THE TORAH OF THE PRIESTS LEV. 1:1-2

God giving Israel the commandments for sacrifice can be compared to a king's son who was addicted to eating meat and hunting. Said the king, "He shall always eat at my table and soon get out of the habit."

Midrash Vayikra Rabbah

1. In this midrash, who is the king?____________________
2. In this midrash, who is the son?____________________
3. Why doesn't the king want the son hunting and eating meat?__
   ____
4. How is "sacrifice" like eating at the king's table?
   ____
5. What habits will sacrifice keep Israel from doing?
   ____

וַיִּקְרָא אֶל־מֹשֶׁה וַיְדַבֵּר יְהוָה אֵלָיו מֵאֹהֶל מוֹעֵד לֵאמֹר׃
דַּבֵּר אֶל־בְּנֵי יִשְׂרָאֵל וְאָמַרְתָּ אֲלֵהֶם אָדָם כִּי־יַקְרִיב מִכֶּם
קָרְבָּן לַיהוָה מִן־הַבְּהֵמָה מִן־הַבָּקָר וּמִן־הַצֹּאן תַּקְרִיבוּ
אֶת־קָרְבַּנְכֶם׃

And the Lord called to Moshe
and spoke to him from the tent of meeting
speak to the children of Israel and say to them:

Whey a person brings an offering to the Lord
You shall bring your offering
from your cows, your rams and your sheep.

What is the connection between the midrash and the Torah text?

____

____

In this sidre we saw that values regarding animals teach us something about the way we need to relate to people. Here are some rules about Tzar L'Ba'alei Chaiyim, cruelty to animals; for each one, write down a principle which can apply to people.

1	It is forbidden by the Torah to inflict pain on any living creature. In fact, it is our duty to relieve the pain of any creature, even if it is ownerless or if it belongs to a non-Jew. ______
2	When horses are drawing a cart and come to a rough road or a steep hill, it is our duty to help them... lest the owner whip them, to force them to draw more than their strength. ______
3	It is forbidden to tie the legs of a beast or of a bird in a way which causes pain. ______
4	It is forbidden to set a bird on eggs that are not of her species. ______
5	If a beast is working in the field and cannot eat any food from the field because it is thirsty, it must be given water. ______

THOUGHT QUESTION

What rules for treating animals could you make up? What could each of these teach us about relating to people?

______

______

______

______

______

______

______

______

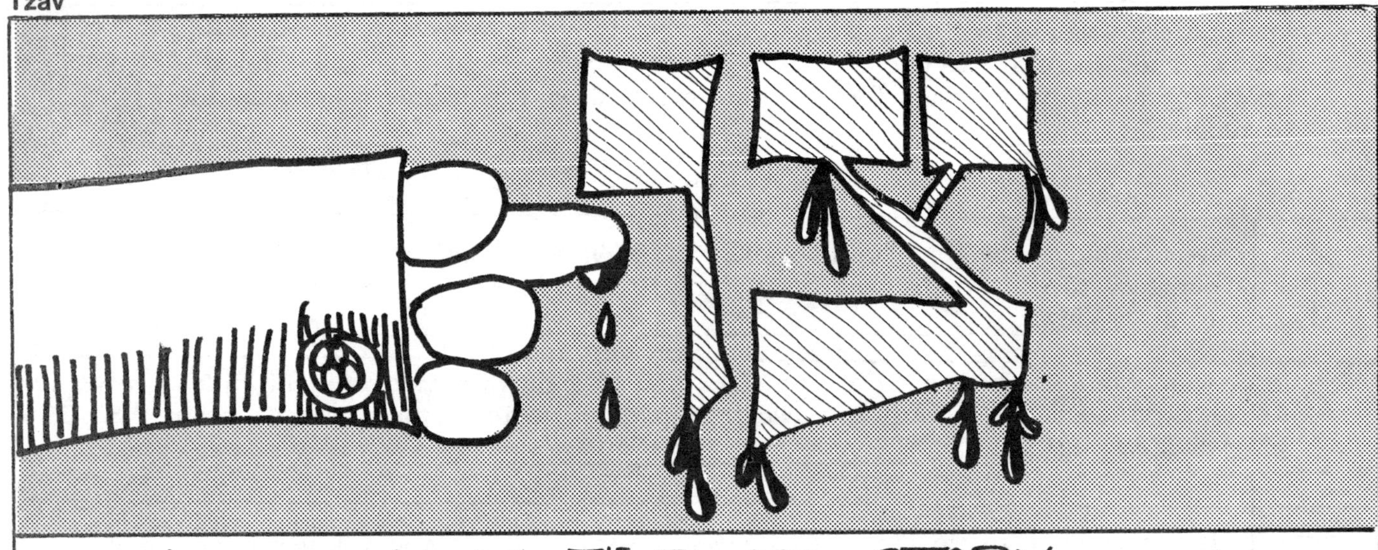

EPISODE # 25: THE BLOOD STORY LEV. 7.26-7

TORAH TEXTS - Write down the value expressed by each of these:

כִּֽי־תִרְאֶ֞ה חֲמ֣וֹר שֹׂנַאֲךָ֗ רֹבֵץ֙ תַּ֣חַת מַשָּׂא֔וֹ וְחָדַלְתָּ֖ מֵעֲזֹ֣ב ל֑וֹ עָזֹ֥ב תַּעֲזֹ֖ב עִמּֽוֹ׃

If you see the ass of your enemy lying under a burden that was too heavy - you may not pass by - but must release it from its burdens.

לֹא־תַחְסֹ֥ם שׁ֖וֹר בְּדִישֽׁוֹ׃

You shall not muzzle the ox when he treads out the corn.

וְכָל־דָּם֙ לֹ֣א תֹֽאכְל֔וּ בְּכֹ֖ל מֽוֹשְׁבֹתֵיכֶ֑ם
לָע֖וֹף וְלַבְּהֵמָֽה׃ כָּל־נֶ֖פֶשׁ אֲשֶׁר־תֹּאכַ֣ל כָּל־דָּ֑ם וְנִכְרְתָ֛ה הַנֶּ֥פֶשׁ הַהִ֖וא מֵעַמֶּֽיהָ׃

You must not comsume any blood - either of bird or of animal in any of your homes. Any one who eats blood shall be cut off from his kin.

These rules come from the Shulchan Aruch - a code of Jewish Law. What are these rules trying to accomplish? What is the value they are expressing?

1. Before the meat is salted it must be thoroughly rinsed with water. The meat should be soaked and entirely submerged in water for half and hour.

4. If a piece of meat is cut up again after soaking, the new surface produced by the cut must be thoroughly washed of the surface blood.

7. After the meat has been soaked, the water must be allowed to drain off, so that the salt may not dissolve at once and become ineffective at drawing off the blood.

9. The salt must be sprinkled on all sides of the meat, so that no part of the surface is left unsalted. Care should be taken to open poultry properly, so that it may be well salted within.

10. The meat which has been salted must be placed where the blood can easily drain off.

11. The meat should remain in salt for one hour, but in case of emergency, 24 minutes will do.

12. After the meat has remained in salt for the proper length of time, the salt should be shaken off and the meat rinsed 3 times.

20. Liver, because it contains a large quantity of blood, may not be made KASHER in the same manner as ordinary meat. It must first be cut open, and then broiled over a fire, with the parts open downward so that the blood may drain from them.

A. WHAT ARE THESE RULES TRYING TO DO? (How do they "put a hedge" around the rule from Leviticus about eating blood?).

____

____

Look at this text from Rambam:

Although blood was regarded as unclean by the idolaters, they still drank it, because they thought it was the food of the spirits, by drinking it a person was able to commune with the spirits which joined with him and told him of future events... The Torah which is perfect in the eyes of those who know it, and which seems to cure people of lasting disease, forbade the eating of blood, and emphasized it in the same way it emphasized the prohibition of idolatry.

What two reasons does the Rambam give why blood shouldn't be eaten.

a. ____

b. ____

Compare these two Torah texts:

Text #1 - Genesis 1:29	Text #2 - Genesis 8:20-21
When God first instructs Adam and Eve about living - God says:	After the flood - this is what seems to be going on:
וַיֹּאמֶר אֱלֹהִים הִנֵּה נָתַתִּי לָכֶם אֶת־כָּל־עֵשֶׂב ׀ זֹרֵעַ זֶרַע אֲשֶׁר עַל־פְּנֵי כָל־הָאָרֶץ וְאֶת־כָּל־הָעֵץ אֲשֶׁר־ בּוֹ פְרִי־עֵץ זֹרֵעַ זָרַע לָכֶם יִהְיֶה לְאָכְלָה׃	וַיִּבֶן נֹחַ מִזְבֵּחַ לַיהוָה וַיִּקַּח מִכֹּל ׀ הַבְּהֵמָה הַטְּהוֹרָה וּמִכֹּל הָעוֹף הַטָּהֹר וַיַּעַל עֹלֹת בַּמִּזְבֵּחַ׃ וַיָּרַח יְהוָה אֶת־רֵיחַ הַנִּיחֹחַ
HINEI - I have given you every plant yielding seed which is on the earth and every tree which bears fruit - this shall be your food.	And Noach built an altar to the Lord and took of every kosher animal and of ever kosher fowl and offered a burnt-offering on the altar. And the Lord smelled the sweet odors.

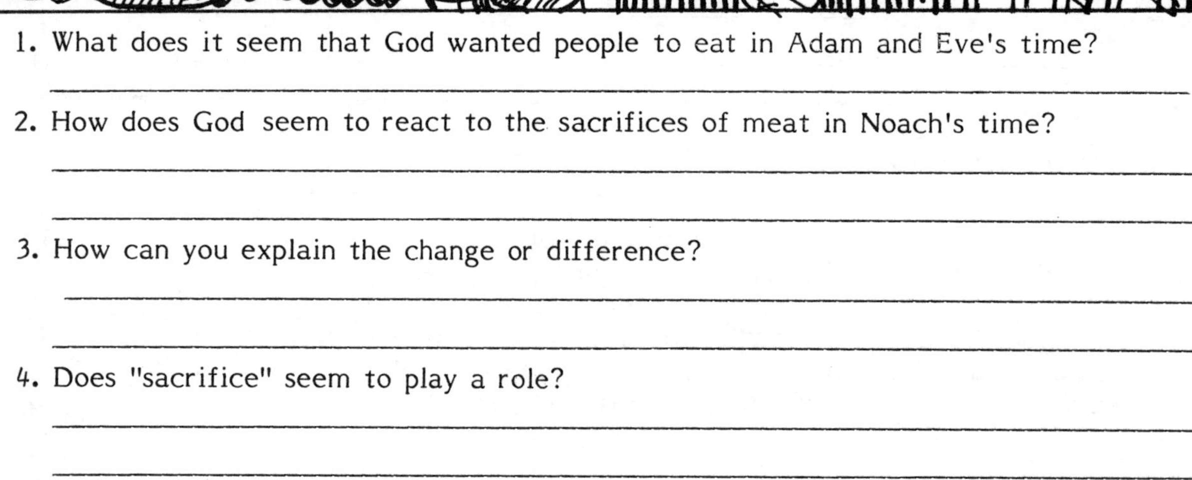

1. What does it seem that God wanted people to eat in Adam and Eve's time?

   ____

2. How does God seem to react to the sacrifices of meat in Noach's time?

   ____

   ____

3. How can you explain the change or difference?

   ____

   ____

4. Does "sacrifice" seem to play a role?

   ____

   ____

Write down 5 important Jewish experiences which have happened to you around a table. Be specific - and write down individual experiences (not just seder, shabbat, etc.)

1. ____

____

____

2. ____

____

____

3. ____

____

____

4. ____

____

____

5. ____

____

____

In thinking about these experiences - what about the table, the food, and the ritual contributed to these experiences?

____

____

____

____

____

____

____

____

EPISODE #26: MURDER IN THE MISHKAN LEV.

וַיִּקְחוּ בְנֵי־אַהֲרֹן נָדָב וַאֲבִיהוּא אִישׁ מַחְתָּתוֹ וַיִּתְּנוּ בָהֵן
אֵשׁ וַיָּשִׂימוּ עָלֶיהָ קְטֹרֶת וַיַּקְרִיבוּ לִפְנֵי יְהוָה אֵשׁ זָרָה
אֲשֶׁר לֹא צִוָּה אֹתָם׃ וַתֵּצֵא אֵשׁ מִלִּפְנֵי יְהוָה וַתֹּאכַל
אוֹתָם וַיָּמֻתוּ לִפְנֵי יְהוָה׃ וַיֹּאמֶר מֹשֶׁה אֶל־אַהֲרֹן הוּא
אֲשֶׁר־דִּבֶּר יְהוָה ׀ לֵאמֹר בִּקְרֹבַי אֶקָּדֵשׁ וְעַל־פְּנֵי כָל־הָעָם
אֶכָּבֵד וַיִּדֹּם אַהֲרֹן׃ וַיִּקְרָא מֹשֶׁה אֶל־מִישָׁאֵל וְאֶל אֶלְצָפָן
בְּנֵי עֻזִּיאֵל דֹּד אַהֲרֹן וַיֹּאמֶר אֲלֵהֶם קִרְבוּ שְׂאוּ אֶת־אֲחֵיכֶם
מֵאֵת פְּנֵי־הַקֹּדֶשׁ אֶל־מִחוּץ לַמַּחֲנֶה׃ וַיִּקְרְבוּ וַיִּשָּׂאֻם
בְּכֻתֳּנֹתָם אֶל־מִחוּץ לַמַּחֲנֶה כַּאֲשֶׁר דִּבֶּר מֹשֶׁה׃ וַיֹּאמֶר
מֹשֶׁה אֶל־אַהֲרֹן וּלְאֶלְעָזָר וּלְאִיתָמָר ׀ בָּנָיו רָאשֵׁיכֶם אַל־
תִּפְרָעוּ ׀ וּבִגְדֵיכֶם לֹא־תִפְרֹמוּ וְלֹא תָמֻתוּ וְעַל כָּל־הָעֵדָה
יִקְצֹף וַאֲחֵיכֶם כָּל־בֵּית יִשְׂרָאֵל יִבְכּוּ אֶת־הַשְּׂרֵפָה אֲשֶׁר
שָׂרַף יְהוָה׃ וּמִפֶּתַח אֹהֶל מוֹעֵד לֹא תֵצְאוּ פֶּן־תָּמֻתוּ כִּי־
שֶׁמֶן מִשְׁחַת יְהוָה עֲלֵיכֶם וַיַּעֲשׂוּ כִּדְבַר מֹשֶׁה׃ פ
וַיְדַבֵּר יְהוָה אֶל־אַהֲרֹן לֵאמֹר׃ יַיִן וְשֵׁכָר אַל־תֵּשְׁתְּ ׀
אַתָּה ׀ וּבָנֶיךָ אִתָּךְ בְּבֹאֲכֶם אֶל־אֹהֶל מוֹעֵד וְלֹא תָמֻתוּ
חֻקַּת עוֹלָם לְדֹרֹתֵיכֶם׃

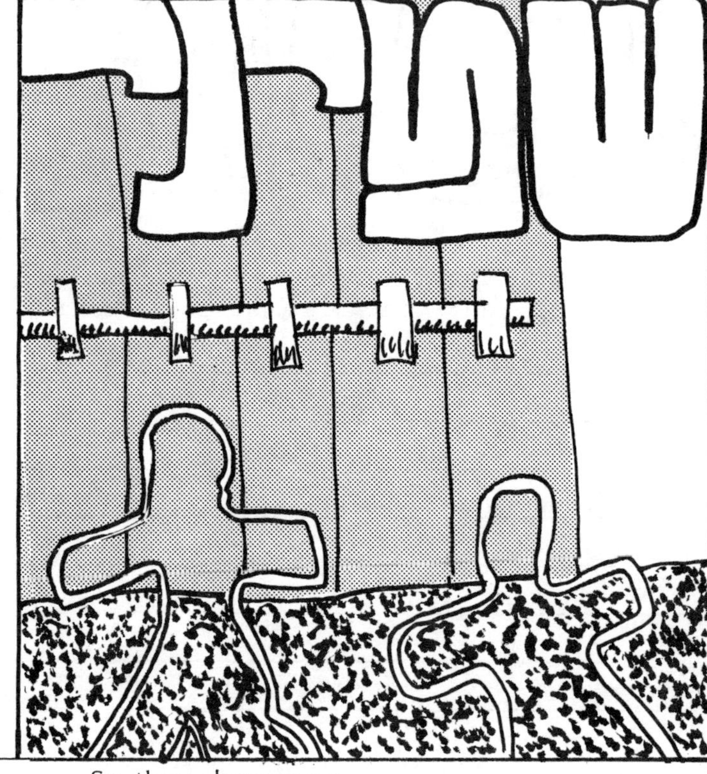

Nadav and Avihu
the sons of Aaron
each took his fire pan
and put fire in it
and put incense on it
and offered strange fire before the Lord -
which the Lord had not commanded them.

There also came out a fire from before the Lord
and devoured them
and they died before the Lord.

Them Moshe said to Aaron:
"This is what the Lord meant when the Lord said:
'Through those who are near to Me I will be sanctified and before all the people I will be glorified.'"

And Aaron held his peace.

And Moshe called Mishael and Elzaphan
the sons of Uzziel - the uncle of Aaron,
and said to them - "Draw near, carry your relatives from before the Tabernacle out of the camp."

So they drew near
and carried them in their tunics
out of the camp, as Moshe has said.

and Moshe said to Aaron and to Eleazar
and to Ithamar his sons:
"Don't let your hair go loose, nor rend your clothes so that you don't die and so God won't be angry with all the congregation - but let your brothers - the whole house of Israel mourn the burning which the Lord kindled.
And you shall not go out from the door of the tent of meeting lest you die,
for the annointing of the Lord is upon you."

And they did according to the word of Moshe.

And the Lord spoke to Aaron saying:
"Drink no wine nor strong drink, you or your sons, when you go into the tent of meetings - lest you die..."

WHO DO YOU THINK IS RESPONSIBLE FOR THE DEATH OF NADAV AND AVIHU? WHAT EVIDENCE CAN YOU FIND IN TEXT? ______________________________

____

____

RASHI'S COMMENT

AND THERE WENT OUT A FIRE

Rabbi Eliezer said, the sons of Aaron died only because they gave decisions on religious matters in the presence of their teacher, Moshe. (Siphra/Erub. 63a)

Rabbi Ishmael said: They died because they entered the Mishkan intoxicated by wine. You may know that this is so, because after their death, God admonished those who survived that they should not enter the Mishkan intoxicated by wine...

1. How many answers does Rashi give to this question?

2. What is the question?

3. Why do you think Rashi provides both answers?

4. With which answer does Rashi agree?

5. What evidence does Rashi find?

6. What quote from the Torah has Rashi's evidence?

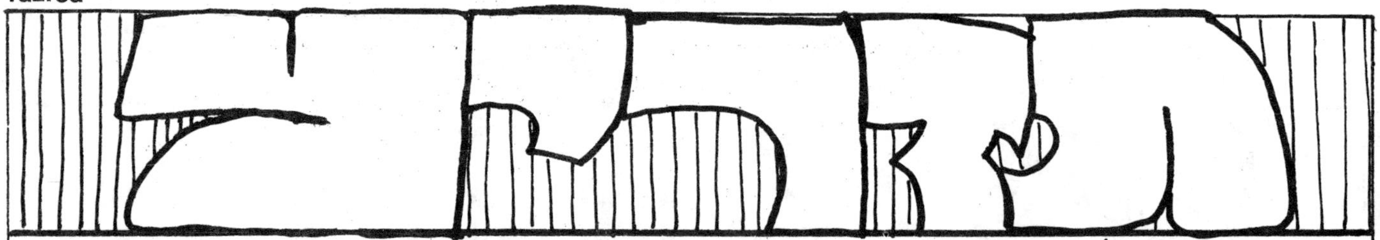

תזריע

EPISODE #27: MAGIC OR MYSTERY

LEV. 13.2-3

קדוש ל

קדוש ל

אָדָם כִּי־יִהְיֶה
בְעוֹר־בְּשָׂרוֹ שְׂאֵת אוֹ־סַפַּחַת אוֹ בַהֶרֶת וְהָיָה בְעוֹר־בְּשָׂרוֹ
לְנֶגַע צָרָעַת וְהוּבָא אֶל־אַהֲרֹן הַכֹּהֵן אוֹ אֶל־אַחַד מִבָּנָיו
הַכֹּהֲנִים׃ וְרָאָה הַכֹּהֵן אֶת־הַנֶּגַע בְּעוֹר־הַבָּשָׂר וְשֵׂעָר
בַּנֶּגַע הָפַךְ לָבָן וּמַרְאֵה הַנֶּגַע עָמֹק מֵעוֹר בְּשָׂרוֹ נֶגַע צָרַעַת
הוּא וְרָאָהוּ הַכֹּהֵן וְטִמֵּא אֹתוֹ׃

When there appears on a person's skin a swelling of a scab or a shiny spot - and it develops into a case of leprosy, then the person shall be brought before Aaron the priest or one of his sons - the priests. And the priest shall examine the plague on the skin - and if the hair on the diseased part has turned white - the appearance of the plague be deeper than the skin of the flesh - it is the plague of leprosy. And the priest shall examine the person and pronounce the person unclean.

1. What do you think the Torah is trying to teach with this portion?

2. What "rule" is being taught here?

3. Why do you think the priests were made responsible for these things?

BAVA KAMMA 85A

Rabbi Ishmael taught - and shall cause him to be thoroughly healed (ibid) - teaching that permission has been granted the physician by God to heal.

And we do not say: The All Merciful smote and will heal.
Rashi

The idea is that perhaps the physician will say: Why should I have all this responsibility. Perhaps I will make a mistake and will find that I accidently killed a person - this is why the Torah gives permission to heal.
Nachmonides

1. What these three texts "learn" from this Torah portion?

____

____

____

2. In what way these texts expand the idea of "leprosy"?

____

____

____

____

ARACHIM 15B

Said Rabbi Yochanon in the name of Rabbi Yose ben Zimra: The spreading of gossip (evil talk) is equal to denying God, as it is said in Psalms 12:5-"Who has said - - with our tongues we will win - our lips are our own - who is lord over us?" Rabbi Yose further said: "Who ever retells gossip is visited by plagues." Said Resh Lakish: "What is the implication of the phrase 'This shall be law of the leper - Me-Tzora - this shall be the law of the one who spreads evil talk (Motzi-Shem-Ra).'

1. What does this text "learn" from this Torah portion?

____

____

____

____

2. In what way does it expand the idea of "leprosy"?

____

____

____

____

3. In the Torah portion - what was done to a leper? Why is this a good way of dealing with gossip?

____

____

____

____

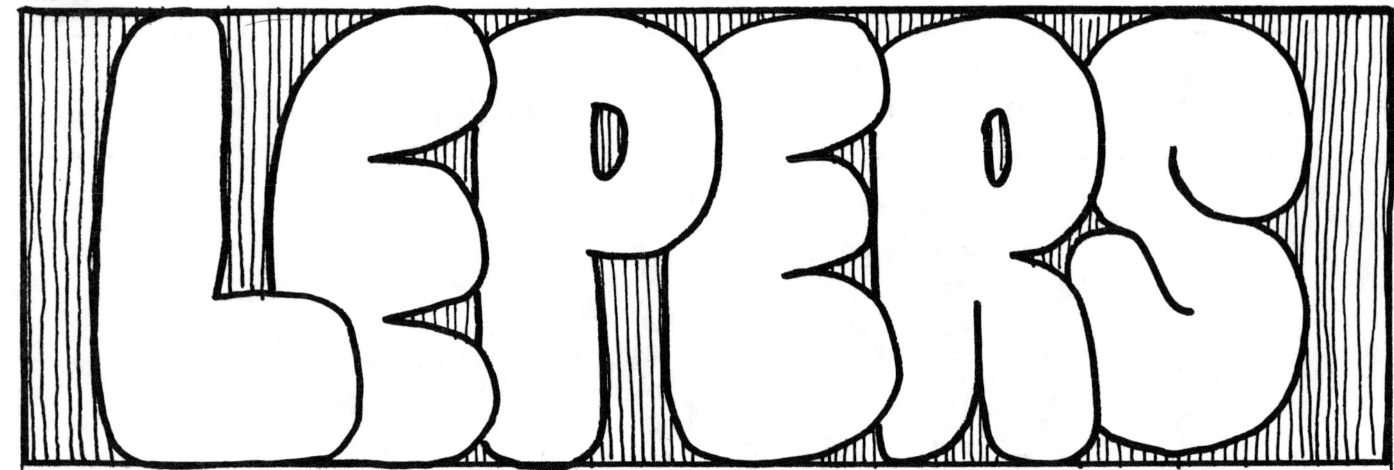

In this Torah portion the text talks about "lepers" and find ways to bring them back into the camp. List 10 groups of people in our society who are isolated and need to be brought back into the camp.

1. ______________________________

2. ______________________________

3. ______________________________

4. ______________________________

5. ______________________________

6. ______________________________

7. ______________________________

8. ______________________________

9. ______________________________

10. ______________________________

EPISODE #28: THE TREATMENT

LEV. 14.1 FF.

The Lord spoke to Moshe saying:
This shall be the ritual for a leper at the time that he is to be cleansed.
When it has been reported to the priest the priest shall go outside the camp.
If the priest sees that the leper has been healed of his scaly affection, the priest shall order two clean birds, ceder wood, crimson stuff, and hyssop to be brought for him who is to be cleansed.

וַיְדַבֵּר יְהוָה אֶל־מֹשֶׁה לֵּאמֹר׃ זֹאת תִּהְיֶה תּוֹרַת הַמְּצֹרָע
בְּיוֹם טָהֳרָתוֹ וְהוּבָא אֶל־הַכֹּהֵן׃ וְיָצָא הַכֹּהֵן אֶל־מִחוּץ
לַמַּחֲנֶה וְרָאָה הַכֹּהֵן וְהִנֵּה נִרְפָּא נֶגַע־הַצָּרַעַת מִן־הַצָּרוּעַ׃
וְצִוָּה הַכֹּהֵן וְלָקַח לַמִּטַּהֵר שְׁתֵּי־צִפֳּרִים חַיּוֹת טְהֹרוֹת
וְעֵץ אֶרֶז וּשְׁנִי תוֹלַעַת וְאֵזֹב׃

The one to be cleansed shall wash his clothes, shave off all his hair, and bathe in water; then he shall be clean. After that he may enter the camp, but he must remain outside his tent for seven days.

וְכִבֶּס הַמִּטַּהֵר אֶת־בְּגָדָיו וְגִלַּח אֶת־כָּל־שְׂעָרוֹ וְרָחַץ בַּמַּיִם
וְטָהֵר וְאַחַר יָבוֹא אֶל־הַמַּחֲנֶה וְיָשַׁב מִחוּץ לְאָהֳלוֹ שִׁבְעַת
יָמִים׃

The priest shall take one of the male lambs and offer it with the log of oil as a guilt offering, and he shall wave them as a wave offering before the Lord.

וְלָקַח הַכֹּהֵן אֶת־הַכֶּבֶשׂ
הָאֶחָד וְהִקְרִיב אֹתוֹ לְאָשָׁם וְאֶת־לֹג הַשָּׁמֶן וְהֵנִיף אֹתָם
תְּנוּפָה לִפְנֵי יְהוָה׃

The priest shall then offer the sin offering and make expiation for the one being cleansed of his uncleanness. Lastly, the burnt offering shall be slaughtered, and the priest shall offer the burnt offering and the meal offering on the altar, and the priest shall make expiation for him. Then he shall be clean.

וְעָשָׂה הַכֹּהֵן
אֶת־הַחַטָּאת וְכִפֶּר עַל־הַמִּטַּהֵר מִטֻּמְאָתוֹ וְאַחַר יִשְׁחַט
אֶת־הָעֹלָה׃ וְהֶעֱלָה הַכֹּהֵן אֶת־הָעֹלָה וְאֶת־הַמִּנְחָה הַמִּזְבֵּחָה
וְכִפֶּר עָלָיו הַכֹּהֵן וְטָהֵר׃

Which of these actions treat the leper as someone with a medical problem and which treat the leper as someone with a spiritual problem.

GUARD YOUR TONGUE

Lashon Ha-Ra is the mitzvah involved in the prevention of gossip. Look at these texts and explain why each thinks that Lashon Ha-Ra is an important concern.

Why is the tongue like an arrow? If a man draws a sword to kill his neighbor, and his neighbor begs for mercy, the man may change his mind and put away his sword. However, an arrow cannot be called back once it has been shot, even if the one who shot it wants it to return.

Midrash Socher Tov

____

____

"Death and life are in the power of the tongue" (Proverbs 18:21). A person's tongue is more powerful than his sword. A sword can only kill someone who is nearby, a tongue can cause the death of someone who is far away.

Erchin 15b

____

____

You are forbidden to relate anything negative about others. If a negative statement is true, it is termed Lashon Ha-Ra. If it is false, even partially so, it is termed Motzi Shaim Ṙa (defamation of character) and the offense is much more severe. It cannot be repeated often enough that true negative statements are considered lashon ha-ra. The most common defense to a criticism for speaking lashon ha-ra is, "But it is true." That is exactly what categorizes the statement as being lashon ha-ra.

Chofetz Chayim

____

____

By speaking Lashon Ha-Ra you violate a number of Torah commandments. A total of 31 mitzvot - 17 negative mitzvot and 14 positive mitzvot - have either a direct or indirect connection with Lashon Ha-Ra.

NEGATIVE MITZVOT: You shall not go about as a talebearer (Lev. 19:16); You shall not utter a false report (Ex. 23:1); Take heed concerning the plague of leprosy (Deut. 24:8); Do not put a stumbling block before the blind (Lev. 19:14); Beware lest you forget the Lord (Deut. 8:11); Do not profane God's name (Lev. 22:32); You shall not hate your brother in your heart (Lev. 19:12); You shall not take vengeance nor bear a grudge against the children of your people (Lev. 19:18); A single testimony is not sufficient to reach a judgment (Deut. 19:15); Do not follow to do evil (Ex. 23:2); You shall not act similar to Korach and company (Num. 17:5); You shall not wrong another (Lev. 25:17); You shall not criticize your neighbor (Lev: 19:17); You shall not afflict the widow or orphan (Ex. 22:21); You shall not pollute the land (Num. 35:33); You shall not curse the deaf (Lev. 19:14).

POSITIVE MITZVOT: Remember what the Lord did to Miriam as you came forth out of Egypt (Deut. 24:9); Love your neighbor as yourself (Lev. 19:18); Judge your neighbor in righteousness (Lev. 19:15); You shall support your neighbor if he becomes poor (Lev. 25:35); You shall criticize your neighbor (Lev. 19:17); Be close to God (Deut. 10:20); You shall revere God's sacred places (Lev. 19:30); You shall honor and respect the old (Lev. 19:32); You shall make God holy (Lev. 21:8); Honor your father and mother (Ex. 20:12); Fear God (Deut. 10:20); Teach your children well (Deut. 6:7); Keep away from a false matter (Ex. 23:7); Walk on God's path (Deut. 28:9)

EPISODE #29 THE LIVING LAW

LEV. 18

אֶת־מִשְׁפָּטַי תַּעֲשׂוּ וְאֶת־חֻקֹּתַי תִּשְׁמְרוּ לָלֶכֶת בָּהֶם אֲנִי
יְהוָה אֱלֹהֵיכֶם׃ וּשְׁמַרְתֶּם אֶת־חֻקֹּתַי וְאֶת־מִשְׁפָּטַי אֲשֶׁר
יַעֲשֶׂה אֹתָם הָאָדָם וָחַי בָּהֶם אֲנִי יְהוָה׃

Perform (OSEH) my MISHPATIM (Judgments) and Keep (SHOMER) my CHUK-KIM (statutes) to walk in them.
I am the Lord your God.

You shall keep (SHOMER) My CHUK-KIM (Statutes) and my MISHPATIM (Judgments) which if a person performs (OSEH) them - he shall live by them.

1. Look at the use of the verbs OSEH and SHOMER - Can you see a pattern?

____

____

2. What is the difference between OSEH and SHOMER?

   OSEH = ______________________

   SHOMER = ______________________

3. Look at the use of the nouns MISHPATIM and CHUK-KIM - Can you see a pattern?

____

____

4. What is the difference between CHUK-KIM AND MISHPATIM?

   CHUK-KIM = ______________________

   MISHPATIM = ______________________

5. What do you think the Torah means by "He shall live by them?"

____

____

____

____

____

We have asked the following questions about this passage. Use the commentaries quoted below to answer as many of them as you can.

1. What is the difference between SHOMER and OSEH?____________________

2. What is the difference between CHUK-KIM AND MISHPATIM?____________________

3. Why does this passage seem to repeat itself?

4. What is the meaning of "He shall live by them?"

How do we learn that one is required to break the Sabbath in order to save a life? Said R. Yehudah in the name of Samuel: Since it is written: He shall live with them..." and not die through them.

Talmud, Yoma 88b

JUDGMENTS - Things given in the Torah which are consistent with human feelings of justice. These are the things which a person would do even if they were not commanded by the Torah.
ORDINANCES - Matters which are decreed by God. Even if it is unclear why we should observe them the text states: "I am the Lord." telling us that God's authority makes these laws.

Yoma 76b

"He shall live by them" - In the world to come. For if you say it means that he shall live in this world, is it not a fact that he must die!

Rashi

Perform means the performance of positive mitzvot. Keeping means the following of the prohibitions of the negative mitzvot.

Torat Or

YOU SHALL KEEP MY CHUK-KIM AND MY MISHPATIM - This is not a simple repetition of verse 4 but is intended to include other details of the law. Another explanation in order to attach the commands of "keeping" and "performing" to the CHUK-KIM and the commands of "keeping" and "performing" to the MISHPATIM. Because verse 4 uses only one kind of command with each kind of commandment.

Rashi

Rabbi Jeremiah used to say: "How do you know that a non-Jew who keeps the Torah is to be considered as equal to the high priest?" The Torah states, "Which if a person performs them..." From this you can learn that even a non-Jew who observes the Torah is equal to the high priest.

Sifra

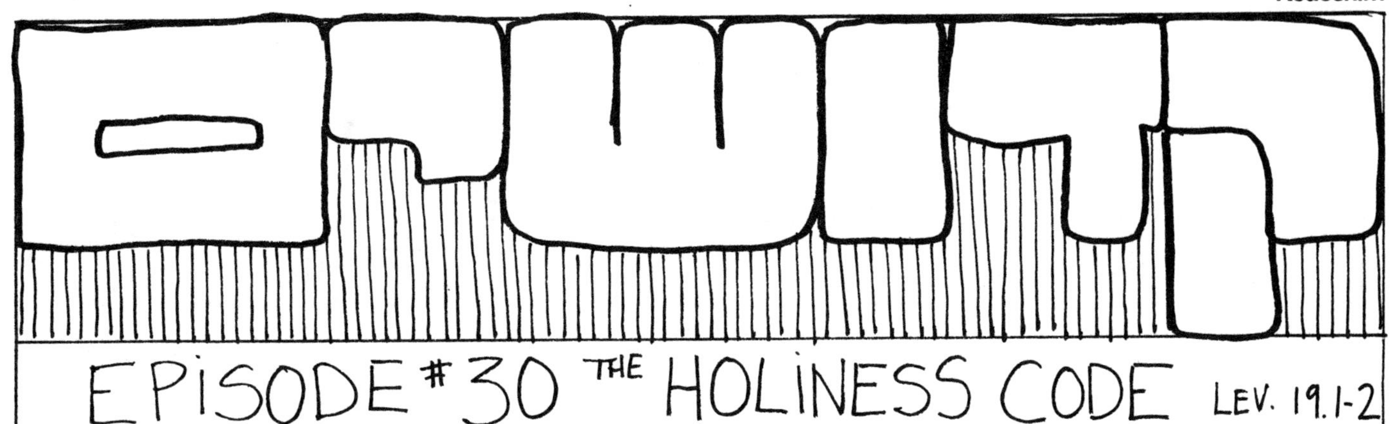

EPISODE #30 THE HOLINESS CODE LEV. 19.1-2

JUDY'S PAGE

וַיְדַבֵּר יְהוָה אֶל־מֹשֶׁה לֵּאמֹר׃ דַּבֵּר אֶל־כָּל־עֲדַת בְּנֵי־
יִשְׂרָאֵל וְאָמַרְתָּ אֲלֵהֶם קְדֹשִׁים תִּהְיוּ כִּי קָדוֹשׁ אֲנִי יְהוָה
אֱלֹהֵיכֶם׃ אִישׁ אִמּוֹ וְאָבִיו תִּירָאוּ וְאֶת־שַׁבְּתֹתַי תִּשְׁמֹרוּ
אֲנִי יְהוָה אֱלֹהֵיכֶם׃

You shall be holy for I the Lord your God am holy.
Each one of you shall fear his mother and father.

אִישׁ אִמּוֹ וְאָבִיו תִּירָאוּ וְאֶת־שַׁבְּתֹתַי תִּשְׁמֹרוּ
אֲנִי יְהוָה אֱלֹהֵיכֶם׃

Honor your father and mother.

What "problem" arises when you compare these two texts?

____

____

a. (CLUE) What is the active command in each?______________________

b. (CLUE) What is the change in order?__________________________

How do these two texts solve this problem.

What is "fear" of a father? It is not sitting in his presence and not speaking in his presence, and not contradicting him.
What is "honor" of parents - it is providing them food and drink, clothing and shoes, and in helping them to enter or leave the house.
Rabbi Eliezer said: Even if his father order him to throw a purse of gold into the sea, he should obey him.

Kid. 31.b.

____

____

____

It is known before God that a child honors his mother more than his father because she pets him, therefore God put the honor of the father before that of the mother. It is known to God that a son fears his father more than his mother, because his father teaches him the Law; therefore God puts the reverence of mother before that of father.

Kid. 31.a.

____

____

____

קדושים

EPISODE # 30 THE HOLINESS CODE LEV. 19:1-2

BENZIE'S PAGE

כַּבֵּד אֶת־אָבִיךָ וְאֶת־אִמֶּךָ לְמַעַן יַאֲרִכוּן
יָמֶיךָ עַל הָאֲדָמָה אֲשֶׁר־יְהוָה אֱלֹהֶיךָ נֹתֵן לָךְ׃

You shall be holy for I the Lord your God am holy

Each one of you shall fear his mother and father
and all of you shall keep my Shabbatot
I am the Lord your God.

1. What "problem" does this commandment pose?

____

____

____

____

(CLUE 1: Find the missing sequetor)
(CLUE 2: Examine the changing persons)

How does Rashi solve these problems?

The Torah places the commandment of keeping the shabbat next to that of fearing a parent in order to teach the following - although I commanded you to obey your father - yet if he orders you to violate the shabbat - you shall not obey him.

This is obvious because the Torah adds: I am the Lord of all - your God - both you and your father are equally bound to Me. Therefore do not obey him if it means rejecting my words.

Rashi

____

____

____

____

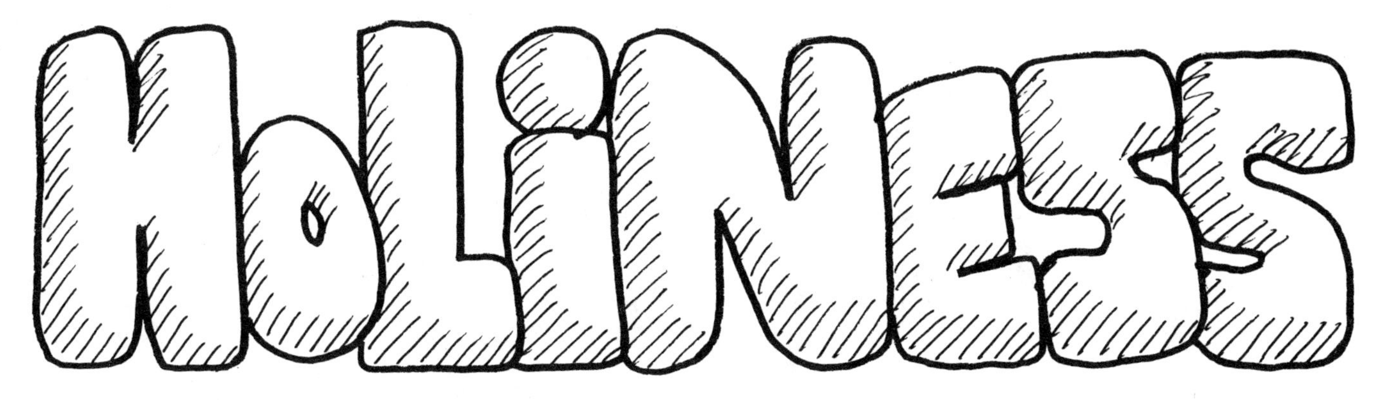

This section of the Torah is called the holiness code. If you had to list 15 rules which would make people holy - what would they be. Compare you list to Leviticus 19.

1. ______
2. ______
3. ______
4. ______
5. ______
6. ______
7. ______
8. ______
9. ______
10. ______
11. ______
12. ______
13. ______
14. ______
15. ______

a. What kinds of things did you list? What was your picture of holiness?

______

______

b. What kinds of things does the Torah list? What is its picture of holiness?

______

______

c. What did you learn by comparing them?

______

______

______

______

EPISODE #31 "THE EYES HAVE IT" LEV. 24.17-21

וְאִישׁ כִּי יַכֶּה כָּל־נֶפֶשׁ אָדָם מוֹת יוּמָת׃ וּמַכֵּה
נֶפֶשׁ־בְּהֵמָה יְשַׁלְּמֶנָּה נֶפֶשׁ תַּחַת נָפֶשׁ׃ וְאִישׁ כִּי־יִתֵּן
מוּם בַּעֲמִיתוֹ כַּאֲשֶׁר עָשָׂה כֵּן יֵעָשֶׂה לּוֹ׃ שֶׁבֶר תַּחַת
שֶׁבֶר עַיִן תַּחַת עַיִן שֵׁן תַּחַת שֵׁן כַּאֲשֶׁר יִתֵּן מוּם בָּאָדָם
כֵּן יִנָּתֶן בּוֹ׃ וּמַכֵּה בְהֵמָה יְשַׁלְּמֶנָּה וּמַכֵּה אָדָם יוּמָת׃

A person who strikes a mortal blow against another person shall be put to death.
A person who strikes a mortal blow against an animal shall make good: A life for a life.
If a person injures a neighbor - as that person has done - so shall it be done to him/her.
A break for a break
An eye for an eye
a tooth for a tooth

In this week's Torah-Toon, we are going to provide no answer, only a challenge. Your mission is to prove that AN EYE FOR AN EYE means that if you are responsible for another person losing an eye - then you are responsible to pay damages equal to the worth of an eye - and not - that your eye is put out. You are responsible for proving that this passage talks about responsibility and not revenge.

ANY OF THE FOLLOWING MAY BE HELPFUL:

1. The climax to the Merchant of Venice by Shakespeare
2. Rashi on Leviticus 24:20 and on Exodus 21:18ff
3. The Talmud - Bava Kama 84a
4. The Mishneh Torah - Damages 1:3-6
5. Other places the word "tachat" is used.

WILLIAM SHAKESPEARE

THE MERCHANT OF VENICE is a play by Shakespeare which involves a Jewish money lender named Shylock. While the plot is complex, in order to seek revenge, Shylock loans money to Antonio on the condition that if he fails to pay back the money - Antonio will give him a pound of flesh. The climax of the play has Shylock in court trying to collect his pound of flesh, and a beautiful heiress named Portia trying to argue him out of it.

PORTIA: Is your name Shylock?
SHYLOCK: Shylock is my name.
PORTIA: Of a strange nature is the suit you follow;
Yet in such rule that the Venetian law
Cannot impugn you as you do proceed.
You stand within his danger, do you not.
ANTONIO: Ay, so he says.
PORTIA: Do you confess the bond?
ANTONIO: I do.
PORTIA: Then must the Jew be merciful.
SHYLOCK: On what compulsion must I? tell me that.
PORTIA: The quality of mercy is not strain'd
It droppeth as the gentle rain from heaven
Upon the place beneath: it is twice blest;
It blesses him that gives and him that takes...
SHYLOCK: I take this offer, then; pay the bond thrice,
And let the Christian go.
BASSANTIO: Here is the money.
PORTIA: Soft!
The Jew shall have all justice; soft! no haste:
He shall have nothing but the penalty.
GRATIANO: Oh Jew! an upright judge, a learned judge!
PORTIA: Therefore prepare thee to cut off the flesh.
Shed thou no blood; nor cut thou less or more
But just a pound of flesh: if thou cut'st more
Or less than a just pound, be it so much
And makes it light or heavy in the substance,
Or the division of the twentieth part
Of one poor scruple, nay, if the scales do turn
But in the estimation of a hair,
Thou diest and and all thy goods are confiscate.

HOW CAN PORTIA'S REASONING BE APPLIED TO AN EYE FOR AN EYE?

____

____

____

____

TALMUD

Numbers 35:31 states: "You shall not take a ransom for the life of a murderer who is condemned to death" implying for the life of a murderer you may take no ransom, but you may take ransom for the main organs of the human body which do not grow back. CLUE: Ransom = paying damages).

Bava Kamma 83b

Rabbi Shimon be Yochai said: "AN EYE FOR AN EYE" means money. You say money but maybe the Torah really means taking an eye. If that was the case - and a blind man blinded another, and a crippled man maimed another, how could one be able to give exactly an eye for an eye. If it was not exact, it would violate Leviticus 24:22 "one law shall there be for you" - a law that is equitable to all of you.

It was taught in the school of Hezekiah: "Eye for eye, life for life" and not a life and an eye for a life; for should one imagine it is taken literally it would sometimes happen that an eye and a life would be taken for an eye, for in the process of blinding the blinder, the person might die.

Bava Kamma 84a

THE TALMUD SOLVES THIS PROBLEM BY REASONING AND NOT BY CLOSE EXAMINATION OF THE WORDS. WHAT IS THEIR ARGUMENT?

____

____

THE RAMBAM

This does not mean the literal inflicting of identical maiming on the guilty person, but merely that though the latter deserves such maiming, he pays the monetary equivalent. For we are told:"You shall not take a ransom from the life of a murderer" implying that ransom is ruled out only in the case of one who maims another...

Why is money indicated in the case of "an eye for an eye"? Since it is stated a "bruise for a bruise" and the Talmud makes it clear that "if a person strikes another person with a stone or a fist... the guilty party shall only pay for the loss of time and for the cost of medical treatment" indicating that the "for in "bruise <u>for</u> bruise" refers to payment and the same is true in "an eye <u>for</u> an eye."

Mishneh Torah - Damages 1:3-6

MAIMONIDES PROVES THIS IN TWO WAYS. THE FIRST IS THROUGH LOGIC. WHERE IS THE LOGIC TAKEN FROM? THE SECOND IS THROUGH LANGUAGE. WHAT IS THE PROOF?

____

____

____

____

____

SOME COMMENTS BY RASHI

וְאִישׁ כִּי יַכֶּה כָּל־נֶפֶשׁ אָדָם מוֹת יוּמָת׃ וּמַכֵּה
נֶפֶשׁ־בְּהֵמָה יְשַׁלְּמֶנָּה נֶפֶשׁ תַּחַת נָפֶשׁ׃ וְאִישׁ כִּי־יִתֵּן
מוּם בַּעֲמִיתוֹ כַּאֲשֶׁר עָשָׂה כֵּן יֵעָשֶׂה לּוֹ׃ שֶׁבֶר תַּחַת
שֶׁבֶר עַיִן תַּחַת עַיִן שֵׁן תַּחַת שֵׁן כַּאֲשֶׁר יִתֵּן מוּם בָּאָדָם
כֵּן יִנָּתֶן בּוֹ׃ וּמַכֵּה בְהֵמָה יְשַׁלְּמֶנָּה וּמַכֵּה אָדָם יוּמָת׃

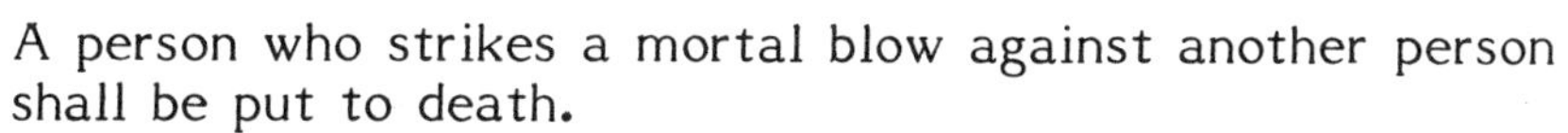

A person who strikes a mortal blow against another person shall be put to death.
A person who strikes a mortal blow against an animal shall make good: A life for a life.
If a person injures a neighbor - as that person has done - so shall it be done to him/her.
A break for a break; An eye for an eye; a tooth for a tooth.

Leviticus 24:17-21

IF A PERSON INJURES HIS NEIGHBOR - AS THAT PERSON HAS DONE - SO SHALL IT BE DONE TO HIM/HER.

Our Rabbis explained that this does not mean the actual injuring of the person but it means monetary compensation. We estimate the injured person's value as a slave and the offender has to pay the difference between his normal value and his value as an injured person. It is for this reason that the word "natan" (to give) is used here, meaning that money was given. (This idea is found in the Talmud Keth. 32B and B. Kam. 84 A.)

Rashi uses two different means to prove that money is paid in the case of damages. One comes from a "higher authority" and the other is linguistic (based on the wording). What are these?

1. ______________________________

2. ______________________________

Why does Rashi use slavery as a way of figuring value?

____

____

וְכִי־יְרִיבֻן אֲנָשִׁים וְהִכָּה־אִישׁ
אֶת־רֵעֵהוּ בְּאֶבֶן אוֹ בְאֶגְרֹף וְלֹא יָמוּת וְנָפַל לְמִשְׁכָּב׃
אִם־יָקוּם וְהִתְהַלֵּךְ בַּחוּץ עַל־מִשְׁעַנְתּוֹ וְנִקָּה הַמַּכֶּה רַק
שִׁבְתּוֹ יִתֵּן וְרַפֹּא יְרַפֵּא׃

And if two people quarrel and a person strikes his fellow with a stone or with a fist and he does not die but has to take to his bed - if he then gets up and walks outdoors upon his staff, the attacker shall go unpunished except that he must pay for the injured party's idleness and his cure.

CONTINUED

AND IF MEN QUARREL

Why is this verse necessary since the Torah already teaches "An eye for an eye". While Leviticus 24:17-21 teaches us that the person who caused the damage is responsible for paying compensation for the loss of limb, this passage teaches us that damages must also be paid to compensate for loss of time and for the cost of medical treatment.

1. What does Rashi's comment teach us about "an eye for an eye?"

2. What is the question Rashi is answering here?

3. What new thing does he teach us about damages?

Put together your explanation of why "an eye for an eye" means paying the value of an eye.

EPISODE #32 THE LAND GRANT

LEV. 23-25, 55

וְהָאָרֶץ לֹא תִמָּכֵר לִצְמִתֻת כִּי־לִי הָאָרֶץ כִּי־גֵרִים
וְתוֹשָׁבִים אַתֶּם עִמָּדִי׃ וּבְכֹל אֶרֶץ אֲחֻזַּתְכֶם גְּאֻלָּה תִּתְּנוּ
לָאָרֶץ׃ כִּי־יָמוּךְ אָחִיךָ וּמָכַר מֵאֲחֻזָּתוֹ וּבָא גֹאֲלוֹ
הַקָּרֹב אֵלָיו וְגָאַל אֵת מִמְכַּר אָחִיו׃

The land shall not be sold absolutely:
For the LAND is MINE.
For you are strangers and sojourners with ME...
If your brother became poor
and sold any of his land,
and if his relatives come to buy it back,
you shall sell it back to them.

כִּי־לִי בְנֵי־יִשְׂרָאֵל עֲבָדִים עֲבָדַי הֵם
אֲשֶׁר־הוֹצֵאתִי אוֹתָם מֵאֶרֶץ מִצְרָיִם אֲנִי יְהוָה אֱלֹהֵיכֶם׃

B'nai Yisrael are my slaves,
they are my slaves who I brought out of the land of Egypt.
Leviticus 25:55

1. What does this Parasha say about the Land of Israel?

____

____

2. What does this Parasha say about the People of Israel?

____

____

3. If the above two statements are true, why did B'nai Yisrael leave Egypt where they were slaves, to go to the Land of Israel where they would still be slaves? What has changed?

____

____

____

The prophet Isaiah picks up on the idea of Israel being slaves of God.
Here is what he says:

How welcome on the mountain are the footsteps of the herald
announcing happiness, heralding good fortune, announcing victory
Telling Zion, "Your God is King!" Hark!
Your watchmen raise their voices, as one they shout for joy:
For every eye shall behold the Lord's return to Zion...
Turn, turn away, touch naught unclean as you depart from there;
Keep pure as you go forth from there, You who bear the vessels of the Lord!
For you will not depart in haste, nor will you leave in flight;
For the Lord is marching before you,
The God of Israel is your rear guard.
Indeed, My slaves, shall prosper,
Be lifted up and raised to great heights.
Just as many were suprised by him - so twisted was his appearance,
unlike that of man, his form, unlike anything human
Just so shall he startle many nations.
Kings shall be silenced because of him.
For they shall see what has not been told them... (Isaiah 52:7ff)

1. What four descriptions does Isaiah use for the B'nai Yisrael?

___

___

___

2. Which of these is connected to positive things?

___

___

3. Does Isaiah see negative things associated with being a slave?

___

___

4. What positive thing does he see coming out of being a slave?

___

___

5. Given all the different descriptions of God and Israel, how do you think Isaiah understands their relationship?

___

___

6. How do you understand the relationship between God and Israel?

___

In this episode we've talked about the relationship between God and Israel as being like the relationship between a Master and a slave. On the High Holidays we use a lot of descriptions of this relationship.

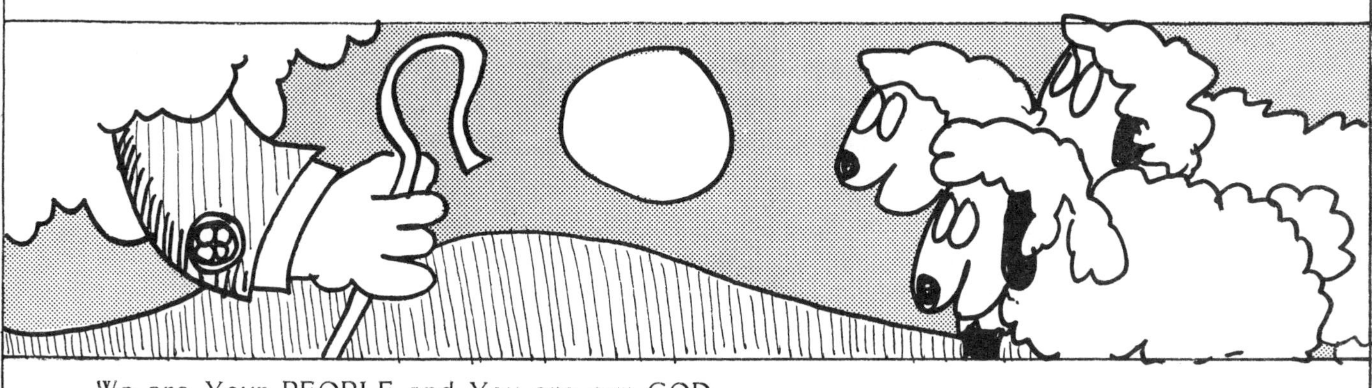

We are Your PEOPLE and You are our GOD
We are Your CHILDREN and You are our PARENT
We are Your SLAVES and You are our MASTER
We are Your COMMUNITY and You are our TRADITION
We are Your POSSESSION and You are our FATE
We are Your FLOCK and You are our SHEPHERD
We are Your VINEYARD and You are our KEEPER
We are Your WORK and You are our CREATOR
We are Your NEIGHBORS and You are our BELOVED
We are Your TREASURE and You are our FRIEND
We are Your PEOPLE and You are our RULER.

1. Which of these do you think best describes the relationship between God and Israel?

___

___

___

2. Which of these is most difficult to accept?

___

___

___

Write 5 of your own:

We are Your ____________ and You are our ____________.

We are Your ____________ and You are our ____________.

We are Your ____________ and You are our ____________.

We are Your ____________ and You are our ____________.

We are Your ____________ and You are our ____________.

EPISODE #33 BLESSINGS & CURSES

LEV. 23.3 FF

בחקתי

Count the number of lines of blessing and the number of lines of curses in this passage.

3 If you follow My laws and faithfully observe My commandments

4 I will grant you rains in their season, so that the earth shall yield its produce and the trees of the field their fruit.
5 Your threshing shall overtake the vintage, and your vintage shall overtake your sowing; you shall eat your fill of bread and dwell securely in your land.
6 I will grant peace in the land, and you shall lie down untroubled by anyone; I will give the land respite from vicious beasts, and no sword shall cross your land.
7 You shall give chase to your enemies, and they shall fall before you by the sword.
8 Five of you shall give chase to a hundred, and a hundred of you shall give chase to ten thousand; your enemies shall fall before you by the sword.
9 I will look with favor upon you, and make you fertile and multiply you; and I will maintain My covenant withyou.
10 You shall eat old grain long stored, and you shall have to clear out the old to make room for the new.
11 I will establish My abode in your midst, and I will not spurn you
12 I will be ever present in your midst: I will be your God, and you shall be My people.
13 I the Lord am your God who brought you out from the land of the Egyptians to be their slaves no more, who broke the bars of your yoke and made you walk erect.

14 But if you do not obey Me and do not observe all these commandments

15 if you reject My laws and spurn My norms, so that you do not observe all My commandments and you break My covenant
16 I in turn will do this to you: I will wreak misrey upon you - consumption and fever, which cause the eyes to pine and the body to languish; you shall sow your seed to no purpose, for your enemies shall eat it.
17 I will set My face against you: you shall be routed by your enemies, and your foes shall dominate you. You shall flee though none pursues.
18 and if, for all that, you do not obey Me, I will go on to discipline you sevenfold for your sins,
19 and I will break your proud glory. I will make your skies like iron and your earth like copper,
20 so that your strength shall be spent to no purpose. Your land shall not yield its produce nor shall the trees of the land yield their fruit.
21 And if you remain hostile toward Me and refuse to obey Me, I will go on smiting you sevenfold for your sins.
22 I will loose wild beasts against you, and they shall bereave you of your children and wipe out your cattle. They shall decimate you, and your roads shall be deserted.
23 and if these things fail to discipline you for Me, and you remain hostile to Me,

CONTINUED

24 I too will remain hostile to you: I in turn will smite you sevenfold for your sins.
25 I will bring a sword against you to wreak vengeance for the covenant; and if you withdraw into your cities, I will send pestilence among you, and you shall be delivered into enemy hands.
26 When I break your staff of bread, ten women shall bake your bread in a single oven; they shall dole out your bread by weight, and though you eat, you shall not be satisfied.
27 But if, despite this, you disobey Me and remain hostile to Me
28 I will act against you in wrathful hostility; I, for My part, will discipline you sevenfold for your sins.
29 You shall eat the flesh of your sons and the flesh of your daughters.
30 I will destroy your cult places and cut down your incense stands, and I will heap your carcasses upon your lifeless fetishes. I will spurn you.
31 I will lay your cities in ruin and make your sanctuaries desolate, and I will not savor your pleasing odors.
32 I will make the land desolate, so that your enemies who settle in it shall be appalled by it.
33 And you I will scatter among the nations, and I will unsheath the sword against you. Your land shall become a desolation and your cities a ruin.
34 Than shall the land make up for its sabbath years throughout the time that it is desolate and you are in the land of your enemies; then shall the land rest and make up for its sabbath years.
35 Throughout the time that it is desolate, it shall observe the rest that it did not observe in your sabbath years while you were dwelling upon it.
36 As for those of you who survive, I will cast a faintness in their hearts in the land of their enemies. The sound of a driven leaf shall put them to flight. Fleeing as though from the sword, they shall fall though none pursues.
37 With no one pursuing, they shall stumble over one another as before the sword. You shall not be able to stand your ground before your enemies,
38 but shall perish among the nations; and the land of your enemies shall consume you.
39 those of you who survive shall be heartsick over their iniquity in the land of your enemies, more, they shall be heartsick over the iniquities of their fathers;
40 and they shall confess their iniquity and the iniquity of their fathers, in that they trespassed against Me, yea were hostile to Me.
41 When I, in turn, have been hostile to them and have removed them into the land of their enemies, then at last shall their obdurate heart humble itself, and they shall atone for their iniquity.
42 Then will I remember My covenant with Ya-akov; I will remember also My covenant with Yitzchak, and also My covenant with Avraham; and I will remember the land.
43 For the land shall be forsaken of them, making up for its sabbath years by being desolate of them, while they atone for their iniquity; for the abundant reason that they rejected My norms and spurned My laws.
44 Yet, even then, when they are in the land of their enemies, I will not reject them or spurn them so as to destroy them, annulling My covenant with them: for I the Lord am their God.

How many lines of blessing did you find? ______________________________

How many lines of curses did you find? ______________________________

What conclusion do you draw from this?

____

____

____

RABBINIC WORKINGS

If we go by the actual number of lines of blessings and curses, it seems that Judaism is three times more involved in punishment than reward. Explain how each of these commentators shows that the reverse is true.

The emptyheaded have asserted that the curses exceed the blessings but that is not true. The blessings were stated in general fashion, the curses in detail in order to deter and frighten the hearers.

Ibn Ezra

The idea behind the material rewards promised in the Torah is as follows. God says to : If you perform the mitzvot I shall assist you to carry them to perfect yourself through them and remove from you all the obstacles in your path. For a man cannot perform the mitzvot if he is sick, hungry or thirsty, in the hour of battle or under siege. These material rewards are thus not an end in themselves but a means. If you have performed some of the mitzvot out of love and by your own efforts, I shall help you to perform all of them and remove any obstacles in your path. But if you forsake and despise them, I shall put obstacles in the way of your performance, till you are deprived of spiritual perfection and immortality. Therefore our Sages taught: "the reward of a mitzvah is a mitzvah."

Rambam

Bar Qappara explained:

What is the text upon which all the major parts of the Torah depend? It is Proberbs 3:6:

In all your ways acknowledge God
and God will make straight your paths.

B. Berachot 63a

אִם־בְּחֻקֹּתַי תֵּלֵכוּ וְאֶת־מִצְוֺתַי תִּשְׁמְרוּ וַעֲשִׂיתֶם אֹתָם׃
וְנָתַתִּי גִשְׁמֵיכֶם בְּעִתָּם וְנָתְנָה הָאָרֶץ יְבוּלָהּ וְעֵץ הַשָּׂדֶה
יִתֵּן פִּרְיוֹ׃ וְהִשִּׂיג לָכֶם דַּיִשׁ אֶת־בָּצִיר וּבָצִיר יַשִּׂיג אֶת־
זָרַע וַאֲכַלְתֶּם לַחְמְכֶם לָשֹׂבַע וִישַׁבְתֶּם לָבֶטַח בְּאַרְצְכֶם׃
וְנָתַתִּי שָׁלוֹם בָּאָרֶץ וּשְׁכַבְתֶּם וְאֵין מַחֲרִיד וְהִשְׁבַּתִּי חַיָּה
רָעָה מִן־הָאָרֶץ וְחֶרֶב לֹא־תַעֲבֹר בְּאַרְצְכֶם׃ וּרְדַפְתֶּם
אֶת־אֹיְבֵיכֶם וְנָפְלוּ לִפְנֵיכֶם לֶחָרֶב׃ וְרָדְפוּ מִכֶּם חֲמִשָּׁה
מֵאָה וּמֵאָה מִכֶּם רְבָבָה יִרְדֹּפוּ וְנָפְלוּ אֹיְבֵיכֶם לִפְנֵיכֶם
לֶחָרֶב׃ וּפָנִיתִי אֲלֵיכֶם וְהִפְרֵיתִי אֶתְכֶם וְהִרְבֵּיתִי אֶתְכֶם
וַהֲקִימֹתִי אֶת־בְּרִיתִי אִתְּכֶם׃ וַאֲכַלְתֶּם יָשָׁן נוֹשָׁן וְיָשָׁן
מִפְּנֵי חָדָשׁ תּוֹצִיאוּ׃ וְנָתַתִּי מִשְׁכָּנִי בְּתוֹכְכֶם וְלֹא־תִגְעַל
נַפְשִׁי אֶתְכֶם׃ וְהִתְהַלַּכְתִּי בְּתוֹכְכֶם וְהָיִיתִי לָכֶם לֵאלֹהִים
וְאַתֶּם תִּהְיוּ־לִי לְעָם׃ אֲנִי יְהוָה אֱלֹהֵיכֶם אֲשֶׁר הוֹצֵאתִי
אֶתְכֶם מֵאֶרֶץ מִצְרַיִם מִהְיֹת לָהֶם עֲבָדִים וָאֶשְׁבֹּר מֹטֹת
עֻלְּכֶם וָאוֹלֵךְ אֶתְכֶם קוֹמְמִיּוּת׃ פ

BLESSINGS

In the blessings section of this sidre, God gives the promise of five blessings if the mitzvot are observed. Categorize each of these five blessings.

I will grant your rains in their season, so that the earth shall yield its produce and the trees of the field their fruit. Your threshing shall overtake the vintage, and your vintage shall overtake the sowing; you shall eat your fill of bread and dwell securely in your land. __________________________________

I will grant peace in the land, and you shall lie down untroubled by anyone; I will give the land respite from viscious beasts, and no sword shall cross you land. __________________________________

You shall give chase to your enemies, and they shall fall before you by the sword. Five of you shall give chase to ten thousand; your enemies shall fall before you by the sword. __________________________________

I will look with favor upon you, and make you fertile and multiply you; and I will maintain My covenant with you. You shall eat old grain long stored, and you shall have to clear out the old to make room for the new. __________________________________

I will establish My abode in your midst, and I will not spurn you. I will be ever present in your midst: I will be your God, and you shall be My people. I the Lord am your God, who brought you out of from the land of the Egyptians to be their slaves no more, who broke the bars of your yoke and made you walk erect. __________________________________

Often promises tell us more about the person being promised than about the one making the promise. If these blessings were important to B'nai Yisrael what can we learn about them?

____

____

What five blessings would be most important to you?

____

____

____

____

____

EPISODE # 34: WILDERNESS ADVENTURES

NUM. 1.2-3
EX. 30.12

שְׂאוּ אֶת־רֹאשׁ כָּל־עֲדַת בְּנֵי־יִשְׂרָאֵל לְמִשְׁפְּחֹתָם
לְבֵית אֲבֹתָם בְּמִסְפַּר שֵׁמוֹת כָּל־זָכָר לְגֻלְגְּלֹתָם׃ מִבֶּן
עֶשְׂרִים שָׁנָה וָמַעְלָה כָּל־יֹצֵא צָבָא בְּיִשְׂרָאֵל תִּפְקְדוּ אֹתָם
לְצִבְאֹתָם אַתָּה וְאַהֲרֹן׃

Take a census of all B'nai Yisrael
Every male by their families
By their father's house
By their NAMES and by their descent.
You and Aaron shall record them by groups
From age 20 up - all those in Israel who are able to bear arms...

כִּי תִשָּׂא אֶת־רֹאשׁ בְּנֵי־
יִשְׂרָאֵל לִפְקֻדֵיהֶם וְנָתְנוּ אִישׁ כֹּפֶר נַפְשׁוֹ לַיהוָה בִּפְקֹד
אֹתָם וְלֹא־יִהְיֶה בָהֶם נֶגֶף בִּפְקֹד אֹתָם׃

AN OLD SIDRE:

When you take a census of B'nai Yisrael
Take it by their number
Let each person pay a fee for himself
and then count the total amount of money
so that no plague shall come upon them through being specifically counted. Exodus 30:12

1. How do the rules for these two descriptions of the census differ? How do they contradict each other?

____

____

____

2. Can you figure out why "This Contradiction" isn't really a contradiction? (CLUE: Look up the purpose of each census)

____

____

____

____

READ THIS COMMENT BY ABRAVANEL:

This census seems to be just the opposite of what the Torah has commanded in Exodus 30:12. "When you take the census of B'nai Yisrael according to their number, then every man shall pay a fee to the Lord when you number them." Rashi explains this to mean: when you desire to discover their total number, do not number them individually but let each one give a half shekel and by counting the shekels you will know their numberr. If that is the case, why did God command them here to be counted by name?

...That counting was because the half-shekel was needed to provide sockets forthe construction of the Mishkan. The half-shekel was not a requirement of counting, for one who fulfills the command of God will come to no harm. This time the counting itself was the central reason. God commanded it without using the half-shekel or any other medium because there is not fear of plague since those who perform a religious duty can come to no harm.

1. What problem is Abravanel commenting on?

---

2. What principle does he introduce?

---

3. How does he solve the problem?

Look at these two laws. How do they relate to the texts we have been studying?

We must take care not to count-off people directly when we wish to determine if there is a minyan. It is forbidden to count in such a manner, even for performing a religious duty, for it is written (1 Sa, 15:4) "And Saul summoned the people, and he numbered them with lambs." It is customary to do the counting by reciting the biblical verse Psalms 28:9 which has ten words in it.

Shulchan Aruch Book 1 15:3

____

____

____

____

The Torah commands each member of Israel to contribute half a shekel each year. Even a poor man who lives on Charity is required to give; he borrows or sells the garment off his back and contributes a silver half-shekel as it is written: "The rich shall not give more and poor shall not give less than half a shekel" (Exodus 30:15).

Mishneh Torah, Shekelin 1:1

____

____

____

____

THOUGHT QUESTION

What new rules or customs would you create from this sidre?

____

____

____

____

____

____

____

EPISODE #35: BLESSING

NUM. 6.22-27

וַיְדַבֵּר יְהוָה אֶל־מֹשֶׁה לֵּאמֹר׃ דַּבֵּר אֶל־אַהֲרֹן וְאֶל־בָּנָיו
לֵאמֹר כֹּה תְבָרְכוּ אֶת־בְּנֵי יִשְׂרָאֵל אָמוֹר לָהֶם׃ ס
יְבָרֶכְךָ יְהוָה וְיִשְׁמְרֶךָ׃ ס יָאֵר יְהוָה ׀ פָּנָיו אֵלֶיךָ
וִיחֻנֶּךָּ׃ ס יִשָּׂא יְהוָה ׀ פָּנָיו אֵלֶיךָ וְיָשֵׂם לְךָ שָׁלוֹם׃ ס
וְשָׂמוּ אֶת־שְׁמִי עַל־בְּנֵי יִשְׂרָאֵל וַאֲנִי אֲבָרְכֵם׃

Thus shall you bless B'nai Yisrael and say to them:

May the Lord bless you and keep you.

May the Lord make His face shine upon you -
and be gracious to you.

May the Lord lift up his countenance to you -
and give you peace.

And they shall put My name upon B'nai Yisrael - and I will bless them.

Based on these verses - answer two questions.

1. Who is really doing the blessing - God or the priests?

____

____

____

____

2. If God is doing the blessing, why are the priests involved?

____

____

____

____

CONTINUED

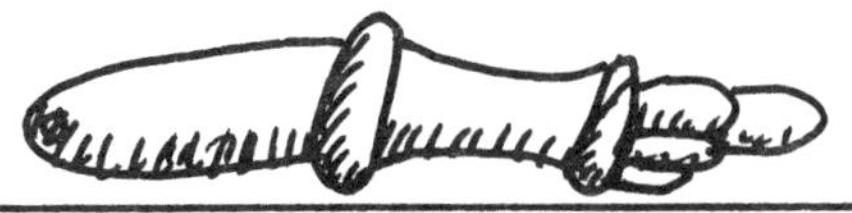

A collection of answers:

God says: "And I will bless them" - this means that the priests bless Israel and I will bless the priests - Rashbam

How do we know that Israel should not say that their blessings are dependent on the priests? And that the priests should not say: "We bless Israel?" the Torah says: "And I will bless them."
Sifrei

Though I ordered the priests to bless you, I will stand with them and together and bless you.
Tanchuma

You might think that if the priests wanted to bless Israel they would be blessed, and if not they would not be blessed. The Torah says: "I will bless you." If they do not bless you, I will.
Sifrei Zota

יברכך ה׳ וישמרך
יאר ה׳ פניו אליך ויחנך
ישא ה׳ פניו אליך וישם לך שלום

MAY THE LORD BLESS YOU AND GUARD YOU

MAY THE LORD MAKE HIS FACE SHINE ON YOU
AND BE GRACIOUS TO YOU

MAY THE LORD TURN HIS FACE TOWARDS YOU
AND GIVE YOU PEACE.

1. Count the number of words in each Hebrew line of the blessings. Can you find a pattern?

____

____

2. How many things are asked for in each line?

____

____

3. What is the difference between "bless" and "guard"?

____

4. What is the difference between "Face to shine" and "Being Gracious"?

____

5. What is the difference between "Turning His face/Countenance" and "Giving Peace"?

____

6. Can these three lines be seen as three levels of blessings? What kinds of things are in each line? How do the levels progress?

____

____

CONTINUED

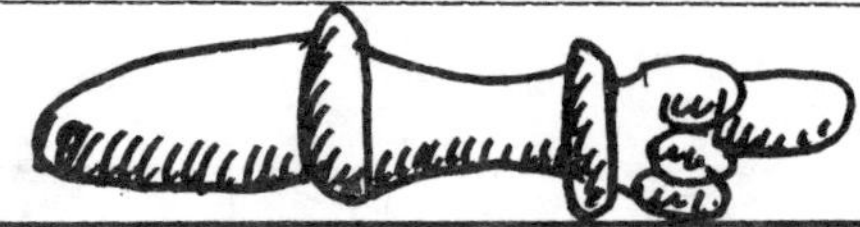

Level One: Bless = that your goods are blessed
Guard = that robbers not steal your property - Rashi

Level Two: Face Shine = The Light of the Torah - Bamidbar Rabbah 11:6

Level Three: Lift Up (Turn) = Removes anger (Ibid 11:14)
Peace = "food and drink is all well and good, but without peace the are worth nothing..." Sifra (Behukotai)

THOUGHT QUESTION

List 3 blessings you've heard given to people in Synagogue:

1. ______________________________

2. ______________________________

3. ______________________________

What kinds of things are asked for?

____

____

____

This blessing is given to the congregation during the Torah reading?

May He who blessed our fathers, Avraham, Yitzchak and Ya-akov bless this entire congregation, and all other congregations - their wives, sons, and daughters and all that belong to them. May He bless those who dedicated synagogues for worship and those who enter therein to pray, those who provide lamps for lighting and wine for Kiddush and Havadalah and those who give food to transient guests and charity to the poor, as well as those who faithfully occupy themselves with the needs of the community. May the Holy One blessed by He, grant them their reward, remove from them all sickness, preserve them in good health, and forgive all their sins. May He bless and prosper their work and the work of all Israel their brethren and let us say, Amen.

Write you own "modern" version of this blessing: Decide what to change and what to keep.

____

____

____

____

____

____

____

____

____

____

____

____

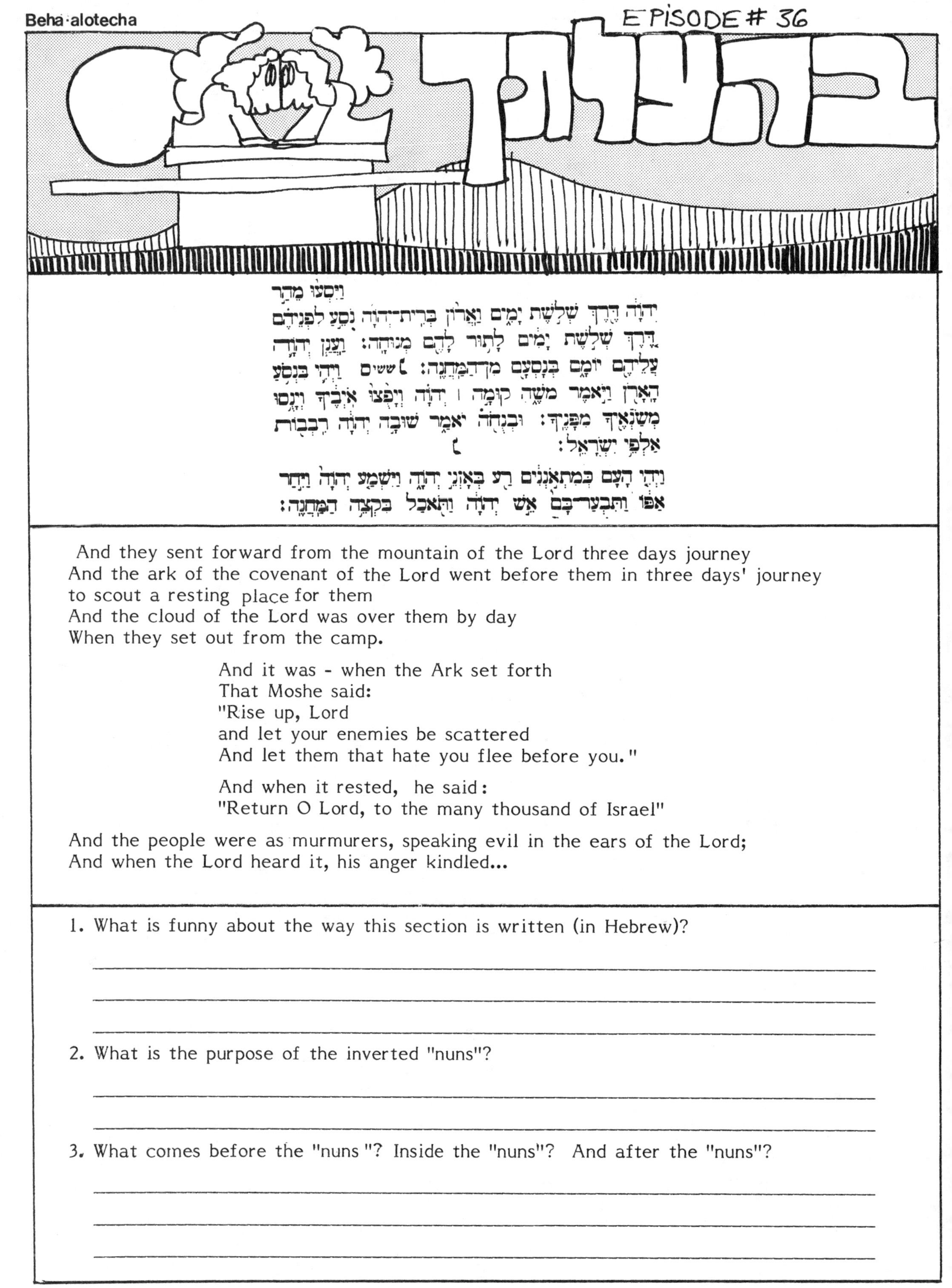

ויסעו מהר
יהוה דרך שלשת ימים וארון ברית־יהוה נסע לפניהם
דרך שלשת ימים לתור להם מנוחה׃ וענן יהוה
עליהם יומם בנסעם מן־המחנה׃ ׆ ששים ויהי בנסע
הארן ויאמר משה קומה ׀ יהוה ויפצו איביך וינסו
משנאיך מפניך׃ ובנחה יאמר שובה יהוה רבבות
אלפי ישראל׃
׆
ויהי העם כמתאננים רע באזני יהוה וישמע יהוה ויחר
אפו ותבער־בם אש יהוה ותאכל בקצה המחנה׃

And they sent forward from the mountain of the Lord three days journey
And the ark of the covenant of the Lord went before them in three days' journey
to scout a resting place for them
And the cloud of the Lord was over them by day
When they set out from the camp.

And it was - when the Ark set forth
That Moshe said:
"Rise up, Lord
and let your enemies be scattered
And let them that hate you flee before you."

And when it rested, he said:
"Return O Lord, to the many thousand of Israel"

And the people were as murmurers, speaking evil in the ears of the Lord;
And when the Lord heard it, his anger kindled...

1. What is funny about the way this section is written (in Hebrew)?

2. What is the purpose of the inverted "nuns"?

3. What comes before the "nuns"? Inside the "nuns"? And after the "nuns"?

RASHI ON THE INVERTED "NUNS"

(C.F. Shabbat 115a) The Lord had this section written with dividing markis (inverted "nuns") in front and behind it, or order to indicate that his is not its proper place. It would have fit better in the part of the Torah which talked about the order of the march, after Numbers 2:17. But then, why was it placed here. It was placed here inorder to make a break between one story of punishment and another.

1. What does Rashi see as the purpose of the "nuns"?

____

____

2. Why is this passage here?

____

____

3. How can you relate the message of this comment to this talmudic parable: This is like a child who ran away form school, because the teacher was going to again warn him about the punishment he would receive if his work was not done right (Jer. Taanit IV 68:4)

____

____

____

____

4. The first wrong-doing is hidden in the phrase - they turned away from the mountain of the Lord - meaning what they learned at Sinai (See verse 33). Where is the second wrong-doing?

____

____

____

____

FIND OUT THE TRUTH ABOUT THE LOST ARK. WRITE DOWN WHAT YOU CAN LEARN ABOUT THE ARK FROM EACH OF THESE PASSAGES.

Exodus: 25:10-16

Deuteronomy 10:1-8

Deuteronomy 31:24-26

Joshua 6

1 Samuel 4

1 Samuel 5:1-6

1 Samuel 14:18-23

2 Samuel 6:1-9

2 Chronicles 5:7-14

2 Chronicles 36:5-8